KT-379-490

A HISTORY OF SILENCE

Praise for *Mister Pip*

'As compelling as a fairytale—beautiful, shocking and profound.' HELEN GARNER

'A brilliant narrative performance.' *Listener*

'*Mister Pip* is a rare, original and truly beautiful novel. It reminds us that every act of reading and telling is a transformation, and that stories, even painful ones, may carry possibilities of redemption. An unforgettable novel, moving and deeply compelling.' GAIL JONES

'Poetic, heartbreaking, surprising…Storytelling, imagination, courage, beauty, memories and sudden violence are the main elements of this extraordinary book.' ISABEL ALLENDE

'It reads like the effortless soar and dip of a grand piece of music, thrilling singular voices, the darker, moving chorus, the blend of the light and shade, the thread of grief urgent in every beat and the occasional faint, lingering note of hope.' *Age*

'A small masterpiece…Lloyd Jones is one of the best writers in New Zealand today. With the beautiful spare, lyrical quality that characterises his writing, Jones makes us think about the power and the magic of storytelling, the possibilities—and the dangers—of escaping to the world within.' *Dominion Post*

'A little Gauguin, a bit of *Lord Jim*, the novel's lyricism evokes great beauty and great pain.' *Kirkus Reviews*

'Rarely, though, can any novel have combined charm, horror and uplift in quite such superabundance.' *Independent*

'Lloyd Jones brings to life the transformative power of fiction… This is a beautiful book. It is tender, multi-layered and redemptive.' *Sunday Times*

Praise for *Hand Me Down World*

'This is a writer who knows how to tell a story, deftly,
surprisingly, magnificently.' *Weekend Herald NZ*

'A masterful, prismatic piece of storytelling.' *Independent*

'An extraordinary novel…Jones is a daring writer who
can be relied on to ignore expectation, and is becoming one
of the most interesting, honest and thought-provoking
novelists working today.' *Guardian*

'Delicate and beguiling. It spirits the reader into a world
that is both fascinating and perplexing. Its charms are
hard to resist; its questions are hard to avoid…
a book of great mind and heart.' *Age*

'Jones's touch is deft yet bold…a novel so fine, demanding
and morally acute.' *Sydney Morning Herald*

'Jones slowly reveals the secrets of Ines's story and its
emotional momentum sweeps us up and makes us
fellow travellers.' *Weekend Australian*

'A fine and moving story with enormous compassion,
emotional depth and tender insight into humanity…
a superbly written meditation on how the disenfranchised
accept the world as it is handed to them, on the weakness of
men, on the deeply moving kindness of strangers, and on the
power of maternal love. It is a beautiful book.' *Sunday Mail*

'We surely have sufficient evidence to trumpet Lloyd Jones as one
of the most significant novelists writing today.' *Sunday Times*

'As complex and as beautifully crafted as a fine
patchwork quilt.' *South Taranaki Star*

'Haunting to the very final line.' *Daily Telegraph*

Lloyd Jones was born in New Zealand in 1955. His best-known works include *Mister Pip*, winner of the Commonwealth Writers' Prize and shortlisted for the Man Booker Prize, *The Book of Fame*, winner of numerous literary awards, *Here at the End of the World We Learn to Dance*, *Biografi*, *Choo Woo*, *Paint Your Wife*, *The Man in the Shed*, and *Hand Me Down World*. He lives in Wellington.

LLOYD JONES

A HISTORY OF SILENCE

A MEMOIR

TEXT PUBLISHING MELBOURNE AUSTRALIA

Reading notes available at textpublishing.com.au/resources

textpublishing.com.au

The Text Publishing Company
Swann House
22 William Street
Melbourne Victoria 3000
Australia

Copyright © Lloyd Jones 2013

The moral right of Lloyd Jones to be identified as the author of this work has been asserted.

All rights reserved. Without limiting the rights under copyright above, no part of this publication shall be reproduced, stored in or introduced into a retrieval system, or transmitted in any form or by any means (electronic, mechanical, photocopying, recording or otherwise), without the prior permission of both the copyright owner and the publisher of this book.

First published in Australia in 2013 by The Text Publishing Company.

Cover design by WH Chong
Page design by Imogen Stubbs
Typeset by J & M Typesetting

Printed and bound in Australia by Griffin Press, an Accredited ISO AS/NZS 14001:2004 Environmental Management System printer

Extract from *Krapp's Last Tape* © the Estate of Samuel Beckett reprinted by permission of Faber and Faber Ltd and Grove/Atlantic Inc.
Extract from *In Search of Ancient New Zealand* by Hamish Campbell and Gerard Hutching reprinted by permission of Penguin Group (NZ).

National Library of Australia Cataloguing-in-Publication entry
Author: Jones, Lloyd, 1955- author.
Title: A history of silence : a memoir / by Lloyd Jones.
ISBN: 9781922147332 (paperback)
eISBN: 9781922148360 (ebook)
Subjects: Jones, Lloyd, 1955—Family.
           Family secrets.
Dewey Number: 920.720993

This book is printed on paper certified against the Forest Stewardship Council® Standards. Griffin Press holds FSC chain-of-custody certification SGS-COC-005088. FSC promotes environmentally responsible, socially beneficial and economically viable management of the world's forests.

TO THE
MEMORY OF
JOYCE LILLIAN JONES
AND
EDWARD LLEWELLYN JONES

...spiritually a year of profound gloom and
indulgence until that memorable night...
when suddenly I saw the whole vision at last.

Samuel Beckett, *Krapp's Last Tape*

Faults may appear to be haphazard, but they
are never random. There is always a hidden
control or reason for their presence...

Hamish Campbell & Gerard Hutching,
In Search of Ancient New Zealand

I'm looking for the face I had
Before the world was made.

William Butler Yeats,
'Before the World Was Made'

ONE

NIGHT-TIME. THE CITY is strung out like sea bloom. No lapping sounds. Just a volume of event that rocks inside me.

Put it down to the hour—that last hour when the dark feels painted on and the shapes of the city float in an underwater dream.

I like to sit by the window and watch the lights come on, as bits of life surface here and there. The shadow of someone appears at a window and then the lights switch off again as though a mistake has been made. The fan extractor perched on the roof of the Irish pub grinds away. In the joinery next door, old window frames and doors sit in a bath of acid. They take a while to strip back to their original grain. In another hour Gib will turn up to open his cafe for a clientele that includes me, and my neighbour, a software designer and chess fanatic, and others less fortunate, who, Gib tells me, are loaded up on methadone, Ritalin, or lithium, or just plain crazy. Soon car doors will bang shut and motors will be left running as harried young parents march their kids into the creche next to the cafe. In certain winds, tiny voices float up to the windows as though blown through a whistle—high-pitched, squealing, so happy to be alive. Down on the corner, outside the music store, the tired old trickster, who has pulled her last van driver in for the night, sits on a bench waving the early traffic through on its way to the airport. I often think about taking her down a cup of tea, like a water-boy running onto the field during a break in play. Immediately below my window, four floors down, the beeping rubbish trucks reverse into the night dreams of those still asleep. Their sleep is delicately poised. A container holding several thousand beer bottles will soon be upended into the back of the rubbish truck, and the crescendo of falling glass will tear through the remaining layers of the night. This is how the neighbourhood emerges each day—modestly, a bit scruffily, in a mix of grace and buffoonery.

I am writing these notes from the top floor of an old shoe factory in inner city Wellington. As a child I wore shoes manufactured in this same building. Then, it would have been unthinkable that one day a suburban kid like me would end up living in a factory, let alone in the city. I would have thought that some terrible event must have befallen me. But if someone had offered me a bird's nest I would have leapt at it. And yet here within shared walls come the muffled sounds of movement, of pipes creaking and groaning into life.

Very little of the shoe factory remains. The old shoe racks are filled with my books, many about famous expeditions. Man and dog and a few frozen ponies. The lone sailor holding his course beneath a sky of terror. There are books that contain shadows. The ones I turn to more often are those that celebrate the unsaid. I like declarative sentences to come with a lot of white space around them. So, naturally, there is Chinese poetry with its inky landscapes. Rice paddies. Bamboo. There are also some sports books, but not as many as I have read. A slender book advises on concreting, and another offers back relief through a series of diagrams.

One or two of these books were owned by my mother, including a paperback in which the Canadian Air Force shares its exercise and fitness regime. It remains unconsulted but kept for sentimental reasons like the jar of jam in the corner of the pantry that I took from her house after she died. There's Evelyn Waugh's *Scoop*, which I retain on the strength of the inscription on inside fly leaf—to Dad from my mother, *For Lew with love Joyce*. While they were alive I never heard love expressed so openly between them. Their bedroom was at the front of the house. The door was almost always closed, which reinforced the mystery of their lives. There were glimpses whenever the door was ajar of two beds parked as in a motel room. An atmosphere so unlived in, so spare, that the rest of the house felt over-furnished.

This is also the hour when the painting at the far end of the room is at its finest. The paint on the canvas is almost entirely blue. Some of the blue is a wash which in places cannot tell whether it is white or blue. There are dark blues that suggest shadows, and a darker fill of blue which at this hour, lit by the one hanging lamp, magically turns into a headland.

During the day there is not much to see. The colours flatten out across the three panels. But at this pre-dawn hour the blue smudge gains in clarity until a headland emerges. Then, you find yourself peering deeper and deeper past a series of headlands to a vanishing point that cannot be identified.

The picture is of Dusky Sound in Fiordland, in the south-west of New Zealand. It was painted by Gerda Leenards. So it is a real place, but in its painted representation it cannot be counted on, coming and going as it does by the hour.

The very same sound was painted by William Hodges, the artist on James Cook's second voyage of exploration. And in one picture, as if to identify and reassure the viewer that this is a painting of an actual place, Hodges has stuck a small party of Maori in the foreground. There they stand, frozen, sculptural. They offer scale and perspective to the romantic splendour of Hodges' scene. But they are also as provisional as a surveyor's peg.

The painting is a cover-up in more ways than one. An X-ray of Hodges' fanciful and probably recollected scene revealed perhaps the first ever sketches of Antarctic icebergs.

Why did Hodges paint over the icebergs? Why would he cover up with this romantic invention what he had actually seen? He has captured the iceberg in the moment, and it is totally believable. The perspective is from the ship's sloping deck. You can feel the silent proximity of the *Resolution*. The two phenomena pass by one another. The eye leads the hand and the iceberg is transplanted onto the canvas. There has been no time to think about the iceberg, no time to ponder composition or the addition of sublime effects. It is a snapshot captured with a grey and white palette.

Whereas Hodges' scene at Dusky Bay is a reconsideration of the seen and experienced. The immediate terrain has been purged of the usual rainforest clutter. Individual trees have been granted more space so that each achieves the elegant domain of an English oak in a field. The scene is up-lit, the light soft and welcoming. The finished picture is a devastating step towards easing the wilderness into pastoral familiarity.

—

Who doesn't warm to the smoothness of wood? Or to a doorstep hollowed over time by foot traffic? Or to snatches of conversation that make the air crackle? When was language ever that fresh? Who said what to whom for the other to say, 'I have never heard that before'? When the wind blows and your skin is wet there is a shiver that is all of a kind, equalling us out among creatures without beds to creep home to and blankets to crawl under. I prefer the elements, and resist the newness and starchiness of the clothes that my mother would like to parcel me up in. I am happier with my socks after the elastic finally goes and they hang around my ankles. The pockets on my shorts are decently torn. The toes on my shoes, issued from the factory I live in now, have worn through. The elbows of my jersey are naked threads. The mud on my knees has dried. I am like something risen from a bog, fit finally for the world I have been born into.

My mother would like to carry out some modifications. I often catch her looking at my hair. She'd like to grab a handful and take a pair of scissors to it. But since it is unlikely she will succeed there, not with my hair, the campaign focuses on my clothing. My jersey, for example, which she resents after seeing hours of her handiwork with knitting needles go to waste. I am a disgrace. She would like to peel that woollen garment off me and throw it out. But these clothes are as close a representative of self as I will ever have. I have the same elemental connection with them as I do with Pencarrow, this finger of land that probes far out into Cook Strait.

This is as far as the lip of the mouth protrudes, the rest is open sea. And of course the natural inclination is to walk to the very edge, and to teeter where the land drops sharply away to crescent bays of shingle and the sea rushes in to make its deposits and claw back what it can.

This is Pencarrow, with half its face braving Cook Strait and its other side demurely turned to Wellington Harbour. I have no idea what the name means other than denoting ownership. Behind it is the older name of Te Rae-akiaki which speaks to where you actually are and what you can see—*the headland where the sea dashes up.* On the other side of the harbour entrance is the other headland, the bottom lip of the fish that *eats the wind*, Te Raekaihau.

Captain James Cook tried three times to sail in through the heads, but in the end sailed across the strait instead to explore and map the coast of the South Island. The day he gave up, a nor-westerly blasted across the harbour throwing up tails of white froth, a mad kind of wind furious with everything in its way. William Hodges painted the tempest off Cape Stephens at the north-eastern tip of the South Island. The perspective puts the artist on a hilltop above the *Resolution* as it bashes its way through a gamut of towering water sprouts. But Hodges, of course, was on board, in the midst of the wild crossing. The picture is full of motion and danger. The artist has thrown the wild elements onto the canvas and then inserted the ship the way as children we place our toy boat gently down in the bath. The painting does manage to convey some of the personal insult felt when battling into a gale. I have never felt as lightly tethered to the earth as when the nor-wester is at full bombastic strength. Even my face feels rearranged—I can feel the nose bone sticking up and the wrong patch of skin where the forehead normally sits. Eyelids have to be prised open. The nose drips.

I understand—that is, I have been told by my father—that occasionally small kids are blown out to sea. I look hard at a speck in the distance.

We have been walking for hours, and it is about time I was given a biscuit. The sheep in the long windswept grass are annoyed with me. They don't look at Mum or Dad. Dad stops to grab at his hat, paws at the wind, and the sheep dart off. The seagulls don't hear a thing. They float above.

All afternoon we walk along this headland in a happy elevated state. It is exhilarating and at times I feel as though some sort of recognition is passing between place and body, one that runs much deeper than the mere act of walking or watching the wind rip through the tall grass.

As the years move on, the walks are repeated, and each time I feel as though I am walking into something, slipping ever deeper inside of the skin of something that I cannot name, a cloaking sensation without the cloak itself.

And at such times, I would have said I felt like I was being guided, but without a guide I could point to.

It turns out that someone painted this landscape too, which is no surprise. But where I found it is—in the display window of a bookshop in Hastings, in England. This was seven or eight years ago. I was in a street, hurrying along somewhere—my marriage had failed and I was infatuated with a young woman and madly in pursuit of something I had shed long ago—when I happened to glance in the shop window. Facing out from a large book of paintings in the display were the crescent bays piled high with shingle and driftwood, and the chipped coastal hills that I had walked along the tops of under racing clouds, just like the ones in the picture, on one of those exhausting days when the only way forward is to stick your head down and burrow into the wind.

I leant closer to the window to look for the name of the

artist and was amazed to discover that the painting was not of Pencarrow but of Pembroke Dock in Wales—the birthplace of my grandfather on my father's side, a figure of lore, as I only ever heard him spoken of as 'the Welsh naval captain who drowned at sea'.

—

Depending on her mood, sometimes my mother will bring out a small mahogany box that contains the past. It is shiny enough to catch every reflection in the room but my own.

There is a trick to opening that box which I will never get the hang of. It turns out that there are boxes within boxes, secret compartments that are tricky to get at.

Inside one of its drawers are some medals from the Boer War and a fob watch that belong to someone called Grandad. This person called Grandad is a bookseller.

I was once shown his photograph, or, more accurately, I remember seeing a photograph of someone called Grandad, a stranger who in fact is not my grandfather or father to my mother.

My mother's father is a farmer, a figure even harder to believe in than this other one called Grandad, since he is hardly ever mentioned. Perhaps just the one time, but it sticks.

There are other, bigger mysteries, such as the absence of photographs of my parents as children.

The scar on my mother's nose is another one of those things

that is hard to explain. She is unsure how it got there; someone threw something at her or else she was thrown against something.

Sometimes I notice the scar. Most of the time I don't. But when I do, it holds my attention. It is a scar from a particular moment, an accident or perhaps a mischief belonging to a world that has completely vanished. It is a curiosity in the manner of a fossil.

My mother has no idea what her father looked like. She never met him. She remembers her mother, Maud. In fact she spies on her, obsessively, although she rarely speaks of her.

In 1914, the year that Maud as a 'fallen woman' arrived in Wellington to give birth to my mother, my father was in the care of the city's orphanage on Tinakori Road. He and his siblings were found milling around the body of their mother Eleanor Gwendoline (death by hydatids) in a flat in Kilbirnie. There are six of them: Percy, twins Gladys and Jack, Arthur and nine-year-old Laura, who is blind from—it is believed—'a sand storm at Lyall Bay' beneath the headland that eats the wind, and Lew, my father, who is one and a half.

While Maud is waiting to give birth to my mother, Laura is sent north to the Jubilee Institute for the Blind in Parnell, Auckland, where she is taught to recover the lost world by making shapes of people out of plasticine. After partially recovering her sight, she is placed in service on a farm in Te Puke. A year later she is sent for by an aunt in Melbourne, and Laura is never seen or heard of again. Arthur will do three years' hard labour for breaking and entering. Gladys will file a restraint order against him visiting her. Arthur will disappear off to Canada, also never to be seen or heard of again. My grandmother is buried in an unmarked grave in Wellington's Karori Cemetery, and forgotten. And Arthur Leonard Jones, the father of this mess, my grandfather, born in Pembroke Dock, Wales, will 'drown at sea'.

I know just a bit more than that about the physical world I was born into, but it also has its mythic layers. The land was originally fished up from the sea. Our street abuts Taita, the 'log jam' in a gullet of land that spills out into Wellington Harbour in the shape of a fish mouth. The shoe factory, fifteen kilometres away in the heart of the city, is located in the roof of the mouth. The motorway connecting past and present lives, suburb and city, is the spine of the fish on whose back I swam into the world.

There are other creation myths to consider. As the last of a litter of five kids, rather than being told about the indecency of my mother's late-in-life pregnancy, I am informed that I was found under a cabbage leaf.

It is the weekend, probably Sunday, because Dad is in the garden in his gardening boots and white singlet. I am also there, kneeling in the rich composted soil on the trail of myth, lifting up one fallen cabbage leaf, then another, a partially rotten one, to see if another kid happens to be lying there. I am fairly confident of finding someone because on the coast whenever I lift a rock I can always count on an indignant crab scuttling away from the sudden blast of daylight or a slimy fish wriggling deeper into the mud. Disappointingly, there is no one under this cabbage leaf, or that one. I look up to check with Dad. Through the thick smoke from the incinerator I catch the smile on his jokey bald head. Beyond his sunburnt shoulder, framed in the sitting-room window, is the watchful figure of my mother. Just then I feel as though I have stumbled on something, or glimpsed something for which at that particular moment there are no words like 'cabbage leaf' or 'rock pool'. It lasts only a few seconds. Then my father begins to laugh. He shakes his head at me. By the time I turn back the watchful shadow has gone. The window is just a window, transparent, catching nothing but the passing clouds.

~

Half a lifetime later I arrived in Christchurch to find a city cracked open like eggshell in the earthquake and where I heard no laughter.

On 22 February 2011 there was a violent movement, like the snap of a shaken tablecloth. A city's past now lay revealed, and it was not as most had imagined.

At the Bridge of Remembrance we stood as crowds once stood at the end of wharves to farewell passenger liners. In such a crowd in Auckland I had seen off my eldest sister, Pat, on the *Castel Felice* to Europe, then a place undetected in my conscious-ness. I had to climb over the back fence to look for Europe. I found it in a geography book recovered from the illegal rubbish tip in the wasteland behind our house. The pages were damp, and they smelt as I peeled them apart to find a flood plain in Holland. As often seems to happen with one discovery, several more followed. Soon after on Sunday morning radio I listened to the story of the boy who stuck his finger in the dyke. It was amazing to think that a boy's finger stood between the ongoingness of life and its devastation.

For the moment we stared up at the glaring white side of the enormous ship. It seemed too big and too heavy to float. It sounded its horn, a tremendous joyful blast, and as it began to move away from the crowd I stared down at the weird and wonderful shapes and figures to be found in the oily darkness spreading from below the edge of the wharf, while my mother waved at the passengers on the upper deck, hoping to catch a final glimpse of her daughter.

At the Bridge of Remembrance the crowd stared at a vanishing city. Even a child who had been quarrelsome up to this point was content to push her cold pink fingers through the holes in the barrier.

The silence was that of concentrated effort to remember how things used to hold together. The place where days or weeks earlier a building stood was now an empty site. The change was abrupt and shocking. How small that space now seemed, too small to hold what they remembered had stood there.

Autumn rolled into winter, and memories continued to diminish until all that was left were a few details—the colour of an office wall on the third floor, a particular window view, perhaps a managerial sound in another office, the singular footfall on the steps leading down to the landing with the toilet where a cigarette could be smoked in the old days, not to mention the coded language of glances that buildings collect and come to know over time. The dreamt-of building continued to vanish over the passing weeks and months. The empty lots no longer caught the eye in quite the same startling way as they did that first time the wet clay foundations found the sky. And by spring, the memory of what had once stood barely competed with the diverting sight of a blackbird hopping across those same muddy foundations.

We had been the last to leave the wharf in Auckland. Mum and I waited, and even though my sister could not possibly pick us out on the wharf beneath the lit city, we stayed put. I wrapped my arms around myself to keep out the chill, and I knew better than to complain. The ship grew smaller, and disappeared altogether. Only then did we turn to leave. At last, it was time to eat something.

~

On a school trip to the future broken city, my classmates and I have stopped to listen to the sound of *click click click*. It is coming from a large wooden house. We point it out to the teacher. He appears to share our concern. He looks alert, then his jaw relaxes. The sound, he explains, is made by something called a ram. A ram is a device to draw up water. We look about the street and find elegant old wooden houses, trees, gardens, but there is no water to be seen. Such is the nature of spring water, he explains. It cannot be seen and that is why it is so good and pure. We stare back at the elegant house with the sober veranda. Its iron roof is cracking in the heat. It is hard to believe that a stream runs beneath it.

We pile back onto the bus and go to a breakfast-cereals factory. There, we file by workers in white hair nets. All of them look hostile. And yet we are each given a free packet of cereal. This is fantastic. No one told us what to expect, but the free cereal is a highlight, no doubt about it. We wander on through the factory with our gifts of cereal until it begins to feel that we are the ones being processed. The noise involved in the manufacture of cereal is ear-splitting. A man in a white coat has to shout to be heard and we frown our way through the history of corn flakes.

It is a relief to get out of there, to the waiting sunshine. Especially as we happen to find ourselves in the 'factory garden of the year'. The garden is on a rise—I can see across the plains to where the low hills shoulder the alps. I have the sense of being drawn out of myself to a more distant place. One day I will turn up to the gate of a farm where my mother's father lived, but right now the scent of excitement is closer to hand. Outside the cereal factory there is a girl I like. Five or six of us are pretending to chase her. We could catch her easily if we wanted to, but then what would we do? She is all cotton shirt and bouncing hair and now and then a shrieking mouth. We are not sure where to touch. We just want to. Then the bus starts up and the spell is broken.

~

How strange to find it was ourselves, rather than the foreign victims we were more used to, fleeing the smoke and dust of disaster. I was watching the aftermath of the February earthquake on TV from the shoe factory in Wellington. And no matter how often I replayed the scene I felt the same astonishment. No one looks back at the ball of dust gathering at their rear. Nonetheless each one in that crowd carries a separate memory of the horrifying moment their world collapsed around them.

It is also clear that the young television reporter has never known anything quite like it. She hopes she will be able to hold her nerve. She must stop people where she can, and ask them what they have seen.

There is a wild lurch. The screen fills with the side of a building, then the trembling ground, now a longer view of the road and the crowd hurrying out of the smoke. And the aftershock passes.

Then a man in a headband jogs into the picture. He stops, looks around, jogs on, stops again. He is on his lunch-hour run, like any other day, I suppose that's what he thinks, and now he doesn't know whether to continue on as a jogger, or a victim or a witness. But, ludicrously, and all this time later, it still annoys me that he jogged on the spot as if waiting for the traffic lights to change, while behind him water mains burst, sewerage systems collapsed, vehicles pitched into sinkholes, houses slid over cliffs, ancient sandhills pushed up through layers of tarseal, and the city's battlements of masonry and plaster collapsed into its streets. At the same time, he offered some reference point because the television camera seemed to inhabit him, and so when he turned we saw through his eyes that enormous cloud of dust and, emerging out of it, a crowd of people. I was surprised by how composed they appeared, but now I wonder if it was shock I saw, that an internal rumbling had frozen them into stately repose as a way of retaining their dignity while their city collapsed around them. Then, at last the jogger succumbed to the moment to look decently confused, and lost. He put his hands on his hips as if at the end of a long race and raised his eyes skyward.

Was it that day, or the day after? An expat BBC radio producer rang to ask if I would write something about the earthquake in Christchurch to be read over the air. He said this sort of thing isn't supposed to happen in New Zealand. And when he said, 'It's like a movie', I knew exactly what he meant, even if he had the disaster genre in mind. I happened to be thinking more about my own relationship to the event, and how a movie manages to juggle notions of artificial presence and engagement with action that is unfolding in another time and place.

The producer asked if I would write about what the country was going through. After giving it some thought I decided that I couldn't—a person in the far north of the country, or for that matter in London, had a relationship with the earthquake that inevitably was different from that of someone thrown to the ground near its epicentre. How could one speak for all? It depended on one's proximity to the event as well as one's inner constituency. My own response comprised a profound sorrow for the plight of my countrymen and, more surprisingly, a bunch of memories that had come upon me in no particular order but indiscriminately, as though flushed up from unsettled sediment within.

Still, it was nice to be asked, if appalling to think about it in such a way. At the time of the invitation the death toll was rising; limbs were being amputated to free people from the wreckage. Now, this morning, a year and a few months after the February quake, I read of a survivor, who had lost both legs in the collapse of the Pyne Gould Corporation building, preparing to take part in this year's New York marathon in a wheelchair. It occurred to me that he was probably lying trapped in building rubble when the producer had called up as you might for a plumber or a serviceable handyman ready to start work at a moment's notice.

I was not the person the producer was after. I was on the edge of my seat, in front of the screen, remote in hand, nodding dumbly into the phone. But he was right to compare the scenes to a movie. They released a personal catalogue of horror that raced to the surface of my being in exactly the same way as those I had witnessed on the unscripted face of the young television reporter—things that I hadn't given a thought to, not for years, events long since buried by subsequent experiences—and I found myself thrown off-balance by this loosening of self.

There on television were flood-lit pictures of rescuers digging with their hands into piles of broken timber and masonry. I found myself isolated by my own memories, some of which were banal, almost unutterable and worthless, certainly nothing to blurt out to the producer calling from London, still there on the line, patiently waiting as my tradesman's thoughts migrated in their wild way through a progression of horror beginning with my first time at the butcher's. The transition from the street, pushing through the curtain of red and blue streamers, is shocking. One moment I am with Mum outside in the summer under blue sky and white cloud and in the murmuring warmth of the footpaths, and the next I am surrounded by bloody body parts with pleasant-sounding names, decorated with bits of fern and parsley. My mother, on the other hand, looks over the bits of carcass as she does when she picks up something at the beach, with a keen interest tucked inside a thin public smile. The butcher's apron, I notice, is splattered with blood. So are his hands which he has slapped onto his hips. I look back at the curtain of cheerful red and blue streamers. I am slowly arriving at the idea of deception—that deception is one of the hinges the world swings back and forth on. The tidy world of asphalt and lawn is out there. In here, butchered flesh. As I remember it, I escaped to the blinding sunshine outside and the promise of a lemonade iceblock. And the carnage I saw around this time. A smash up by Waterloo Bridge in the Hutt. Two mangled bits of steel, an amazing amount of broken glass, the smell of petrol, a tide of human blood—and the slow wailing sirens and the pointlessness of the policeman alone at the scene pushing at the air with his hands.

And then, in a calmer moment, after I'd told the producer I would get back to him and had put the phone down, I sat stone still, struck by something unexpected and heard again, I suppose for the tenth, twentieth or hundredth time—the gun shot. The episode unfolds always in the same way. I look at the clock. And seeing it is 2 a.m. feel a bit sour. I pull on a pair of jeans and a shirt. The apartment is in the Western Addition, one of the dodgier neighbourhoods of San Francisco. I have heard that the cops don't like to come here at night. But, down on the street, there they are. A police car has driven up onto the footpath. Two cops are shining torches in the window of the Palestinian corner store. A black man is sitting on the edge of the footpath. He looks up at me. His eyes are glassy. Then I notice the red hole in the chest of his white shirt. It occurs to me that I have seen this before, and I have, perhaps a hundred or maybe even a thousand times before, to the point where it ceases to shock, and I have forgotten how to feel. The instinctive horror I felt the first time I entered the butcher shop has exhausted itself. So when the producer said of the earthquake, 'It's just like a movie', I did know what he meant, except this time it was different.

~

This was a real disaster. Equally, it was plain to see that it had come out of an unacknowledged past. The old maps clearly spelt out the swamp and wetland history of the city's foundations. But that had been overlooked or perhaps was thought to have been triumphed over by advances in swamp-draining techniques, then covered up with concrete and bitumen.

Within days of the earthquake, posters advising drop off points for clothes and food and other supplies went up on walls and lampposts across Wellington.

One lunch hour I joined a long line of people at the entrance-way to Pipitea Marae to drop off a couple of cartons of men's razors and toiletries that I'd been told were in short supply. The organisation and efficiency of the operation were impressive. Everyone seemed to know instinctively what to do. An older Maori woman came up to me and inquired compassionately, 'Where are you from, dear?' A number of people escaping Christchurch, including foreign tourists, had spent the night in the marae on their way north. I think she had confused me with one of them. I was sorry to disappoint her. I was only here to help. Then she asked if she could make me a cup of tea. She too wanted to help—anyone that she could. I politely declined, and she said, 'God bless you.'

A few days after the massive Napier earthquake in 1931 my father cycled 385 kilometres to help with the clean up. I had always known this, although like many things that I know I don't remember ever being told. It was one of those things one absorbs, like knowing the sky is filled with stars, without the need of someone pointing it out.

For several weeks I mulled over going down to Christchurch to pitch in, but then I heard about a 'student army of ten thousand' conscripted over Facebook and felt discouraged. Ten thousand pairs of youthful hands, each with a spade to shovel up the silted streets and driveways. And there they appeared, onscreen and in newspaper photographs. They were magnificent. And I felt done out of a job.

Then I thought, I should go anyway. At the very least I could help pick up things that had been broken. Or maybe I could take a shovel down with me and join the student army, but the idea of a twenty-year-old on the end of a shovel held me back. My father, it occurred to me, had been about the same age as the students when he pedalled all the way up to Napier.

Within months of the Christchurch earthquake, the old buildings in the run-down and slightly louche but lively Cuba Street precinct around the shoe factory in Wellington were red-stickered—they had been judged unsafe to inhabit because their structural robustness fell below the required standard to survive a severe earthquake. House-buyers now avoided brick dwellings, and were anxious more than ever to know how well their prospective purchase would stand up to a Christchurch-sized quake in Wellington.

This transference of anxiety was understandable in a city repeatedly told that an earthquake of apocalyptic proportion is overdue. Since I was in primary school we have been in rehearsal. I remember in earthquake drill waiting for my imminent demise with breath held and eyes wide. I didn't want to miss any of it, especially not the signal from the teacher that my world was about to change. At a clap of his hands we dropped beneath our desks. After one minute, which always felt longer, there was another clap of the hands and we climbed back up and glanced around at one another: happy survivors.

My anxieties prompted by the quake in Christchurch were old ones from another time and place.

And as emotion swept the country between those who had first-hand experience of the event and those of us who might be described as witnesses, we found ourselves in an overlapping realm similar to the effect geologists describe as an echoing between soft and hard surfaces.

I decided to go to Christchurch five weeks after the quake.

~

Like William Hodges glimpsing the staggering sight of the icebergs at latitudes further south than Cook had ever sailed before, I was drawn and compelled by a sense of awe—in my case, however, for the scenes of devastation.

I had flown into Christchurch airport many times before, and usually went directly to a hotel in the city. I never bothered to look out the side window, at least not until the taxi joined the traffic on the sweep around Hagley Park, and then I would sit up and look properly at the enormous oak trees and the stately space they commanded.

This time was different. It was strangely, electrifyingly different. Within minutes of leaving the airport I saw a tank rumbling along Memorial Avenue. Its tall aerial radiated an urgency that made the houses it passed appear small and needy. And then the randomness of the violence became clear. On the approach to Hagley Park I saw trees stuck at odd angles, like arrows dropped out of the sky from an archer's bow, and a vast armada of rescue and aid-worker tents and motor campers.

A short way on the traffic slowed; the road was ripped and torn, and through the open window I could smell the liquefied earth. Holes, subsidence everywhere. Rubble of every kind and so many surprising sights—the not quite right and at the same time not wholly inappropriate sight of the sky pouring in through the shattered roof of a church. Roads sagged and fell away into fissures and cracks. At the intersection of streets leading into the CBD, young faces belonging to Territorials turned away inquisitive motorists or those who had perhaps forgotten that the old route was no longer possible. And then the buildings, bits fallen off, windows broken, slippages. That world was more frail than anyone could have guessed, to the point where after several trips, it began to look fake, to feel as though everyone had been living in a theatre set.

As the partially destroyed buildings began to come down, the empty sites began to add up, and the edges of the city's erasure spread. Out at Bottle Lake, a substitute city—of rubble—grew. Mountains of the city's debris were being compressed down by graders that sat like toys on top of the heap of piled redundancy.

And then, like Hodges, I found myself seeking to overlay what I had seen with a story I'd heard.

The hairdresser was in her twenties. Her hair was red, I think, with a raccoon stripe of green. As she circled me with the clippers I had the impression of a small animal. *Snip. Snip.* She continued. Her aunt—*snip, snip*—had broken her leg a few weeks before the earthquake. And, she said, her leg was still in plaster when the quake lowered the corner of the house where the bathroom and toilet were situated. So, *snip, snip,* she could no longer use the loo. She said her aunt's husband had cut a hole in the bottom of a beach chair and positioned it over a hole he dug in the backyard.

I was onto my third or fourth trip to the city, and I no longer paid attention to the world outside the taxi side window.

The driver kept looking in his rear mirror for me to instruct him. I waved him on past the Daily Donut with half its front fallen away and an oblong of sky where the door had flown out, past a massage parlour that was a pile of rubble with a flickering light next to a handwritten sign: *Yes, we are still open.* We moved on towards the spreading sky in the east to the suburbs badly affected by liquefaction—a likely address I thought to locate the hairdresser's aunt's story.

The taxi driver pulled over by a line of grungy shops. It seemed as good a place as any.

I got out and began to walk, without any real sense of direction, except to take care where raw sewage ran across driveways. The same sights were repeated—abandonment,

27

absences of every kind. Even in streets that did not appear to be badly damaged, new indignities had been invented. People had dug up their lawn to shit or if they had the stomach for it they shat into plastic bags which could be sealed with a twist and dumped in the shiny green human waste disposal units dotted along the streets.

I didn't have a map with me, but much of the place I recognised from what I had seen on television—the silted footpaths, the slurry grey filth in the driveways, the hard-bitten lawns, the grim occupancy of council flats and state houses. Amazingly, the flowers kept growing despite all that had happened. A large Polynesian woman knelt on a lawn yakking into a mobile and pulling weeds with her free hand. Weeding seemed such an odd thing to do. I wanted to call out hello, to engage her, and say something. I wasn't sure what, but I was thinking, 'This is what people used to do.' Now it seemed to be completely beside the point. The neighbouring houses were empty, and they shook as generators in the street roared to clear drains of sludge and diggers and graders dug and clawed at the road.

I carried on, looking for an address to place the hairdresser's story. I walked in circles for several hours and eventually found myself at the waterfront, at New Brighton, and there on the esplanade I came upon an abandoned couch. An elderly woman had sat down on it to rest. A small dog sat by her feet. I studied this scene from the sandhills above the road until through the alchemy of imagination it turned into something else in my notebook. This account finds me dropping down from the sandhills and crossing the road to sit on the couch next to an enormously fat man. I decided to change the husband of the hairdresser's aunt into a neighbour, an extremely obese fellow whose past as a thin man has been erased and overtaken by layers of flesh. In a city pole-axed by the quake a makeshift toilet will be regarded as a bouquet. At the hour of need the fat man will leave his house next door to the Polynesian woman I had seen weeding, and haul himself, huffing and puffing, into the army-patrolled area of New Brighton to steal a beach chair and then fashion it into a toilet for the hairdresser's aunt.

I still have notes to that effect. In this account his conscience finds him a few days later wishing to make a reparation. The fat man rises every now and then from the couch to look up and down the street for the old woman with the dog from whom he stole or borrowed the beach chair for a makeshift dunny. *He sat down heavily. His breath was drawn up from a pit of broken timbers. His eyes followed his breath into his lungs. After a fourth or fifth breath his eyes began to move and notice things. I leant closer to hear the man speak. For he spoke in a whisper as though he was unused to being heard. When he stopped speaking he sat with his feet splayed and a hand on each thigh, with an inviolable sense of occupancy, like a hen sitting on its eggs.*

~

I left the beach and retraced my way through the gardening woman's neighbourhood. The windows jarred with late afternoon light. There were more trucks and graders shuffling and reversing. Their noise and the acrid smell of silt would pursue me all the way into sleep that night. But there, in the midst of it all, I saw the small rose garden, and the woman I'd seen labouring between aftershocks to cut stems and tend the beds. It was extraordinary enough for me to make a note. But the next day, the observation seemed flat and unexceptional. The touching part was this idea of gardening as an act of devotion. But that isn't what I had written.

Still, just as the sight of one church or ruin can recall another, seeing that woman crouched before her flowerbed brought back the memory of another scratchy lawn towards the end of summer, of front windows filled with a blinding light that prevented the casual passer-by from seeing in. I was back in the street of my childhood, one not that dissimilar to the one where the woman was gardening, and filled with the same idleness.

I am trying to remember other events, sights, thoughts from that day spent in Christchurch's eastern suburbs. The street I happened to be in was called Eureka Street, almost too corny to mention but I will because it is true. My search for a house in which to locate the hairdresser's story was a kind of echo of Hodges' vision with its imaginative element. I had carried the hairdresser's story for the same reasons too—for perspective, to lend authority to that perspective, and to make what I had to say somehow truer.

I could feel my grip on the hairdresser's story beginning to slip, and when I returned to the neighbourhood the next day I found myself looking wildly around for something to replace it, some other source of authority, and seeing the postie on his bike coming from the direction of the primary school, I crossed the road to intercept him.

The woman weeding looked up, and back over her shoulder. She must have been aware of me the whole time. A couple of birds looked down from the pylons. Orange feet, black feathers. I remember the same aspect from somewhere else, jammed up with concrete. The postie shuffled nearer on his bike.

It was five or six weeks after the February earthquake and the moment he'd been thrown from his bike was still fresh. And, as I thought at the time, he will never forget it. Perhaps this is why he was happy to talk. He was quick to say this wasn't his chosen vocation. He'd downsized himself from a previous position in management—it was in some area that I didn't quite catch. We looked to be of similar age. I wonder if that was what encouraged him. He was into his second week on the job when the quake struck, and in this same street. He paused, and we both looked up the street at the tan-coloured port hills. I imagine he had told this story many times. Certainly he had lived through it a thousand times.

He recounted slowly and with care the instant in which he was thrown off his bike to land on his arse on the pavement. As he looked up, the road rolled away from him. Some sort of subterranean snake-like force beneath the bitumen undulating into the distance. Almost in the same moment the same stretch of road sank beneath filthy, greyish, swamp-smelling water. That's when he heard the pinging. He looked up to see the last of the overhead powerlines snap, and as they brushed the swamp water that had risen with such surprising ease, the air turned electric blue. I asked a few questions, then some more. He repeated what he had already told me, but I liked hearing it again. The first time it was such an extraordinary thing to hear that I had to concentrate on retaining what he said. He didn't mind me taking notes. He didn't ask why I did that. Two more birds had joined those on the pylons. The postie looked at me, with both hands on the handlebars now. But I couldn't let him go just yet. There must be more. So I asked him to describe the effect of the powerlines brushing the water and he told me again how the air turned blue. At the next pause we stared at the nearest patch of road. It was grey, intact, a rebuttal of the dissolution of the world I had just heard depicted. The postie must have had a similar thought because he repeated the bit about the road rolling away from him and the sudden and spectacular eruption of the silted swamp water. He looked up at the powerlines. Two of the birds gazed inquiringly down at us.

Across the road the woman stood up and shouted at a small boy to get away from the sewage. The postie pushed his bike half a wheel on. I couldn't think of another question. Then a white station wagon slowed down and stopped. A woman wound down the driver's window and called out a forwarding address. The postie made a note of it, and the woman drove off. I thanked him and by the time I had crossed to the gardener's side of the road I had let go of the fat man for good. He just floated away from my consciousness like a giant advertising blimp. I remember feeling curiously light and unburdened, as silly as a feather, because now I could stop my search for an address for him and for the aunt and abandon the notes I had taken down from his perspective.

—

One afternoon I found myself on Barbadoes Street, in the city, assessing the damage done to the Cathedral of the Blessed Sacrament. It was a ragged sight, and yet it retained patches of beauty. A cordon had been placed around it. So I walked up and down for different views. In the autumnal afternoon it lit up with the brave endeavour of a faded beauty. I counted twelve shipping containers placed on top of one another to provide a splint for its street-facing crumbling side to lean against, cushioned by hay bales. At the end of a crane, a platform supporting stonemasons dangled over the cathedral's dome.

Stone by stone the basilica was being dismantled in order to be put back together again. Each stone was painted with a number and laid with care onto pallets spread over the ground at the back of the building.

In its retelling, the basilica would hold true. Presumably in time it would be as good as new, and it would be impossible to know what it had been through. It would give the sunny impression of being outside history.

While I stood at the cordon, people came and went. Cars

pulled up. People jumped out with cameras. A woman threw breadcrumbs over the barrier for the pigeons who had made homes in the hay bales. I was aware of the activity, but more interested in the numbered stones, their carefully preserved sequence of place and belonging.

On repeat visits to Christchurch that winter, I always seemed to end up in Barbadoes Street. It was as though an undertow brought me back each time.

I kept thinking about those numbered stones, until some purpose began to take shape. I began to wonder if I might retrace and recover something of my own past, and reassemble it in the manner of the basilica. It was a matter of looking to see if any of the original building blocks remained, and where I might find them.

I looked at the blocks on the pallet and then at the holes they had been shaken out of. My thoughts shifted in their own surprising way, and for the first time in a long while I found myself thinking about the epilepsy of my youngest sister, Lorraine.

Her fits were shocking to witness—even the seventh and eighth time. The thrashing over the kitchen floor, the foaming at the mouth. The first time, I hid behind the washhouse door listening to her heels banging against the lino.

As with the first trip to the butcher's, I was not mentally prepared. I was five or six years old, and the noise from the other side of the door was terrifying. The high whine of her voice was like a needle stuck on a vinyl record.

At last it stopped, and I peered around the door to find my sister sitting up, Mum crouched beside her. A ring of foam is around her mouth. She has a faraway look. She is not quite back from wherever she has been. I can tell by her eyes that she has no idea that she is dribbling. She would be horrified to know. She is still drifting back into herself. It is a strange thing to witness, like seeing a flower unfurl on a time-release camera. I don't think my mother is aware that I am there.

The fits tend to happen first thing in the morning. And because Lorraine has to set off for work at an early hour, I am usually still in bed when there is a knock on the door—the hour, of course, gives it away—and I hear the polite voice of a stranger.

She's had another fit, this time at the railway station, and in the open door my sister's head droops against the man's coated shoulder.

After a cup of tea and some breakfast, my sister slowly pieces herself back together. She buttons up her coat and stands on the porch ready to begin all over again the journey to her job at a photograph-processing lab in the city.

A graph of seismic activity looks remarkably like a scan of the human brain when it experiences an epileptic fit. The steady cursive waves suddenly spike.

We never knew when it would strike. Something inhabiting her—an evil spirit as it was thought of in the dark ages—decides when it will erupt. My sister is buttering her toast. Mum is looking at her in a certain way, as though this exercise in control and normality is as much an abnormality, knowing that other defining moment is always there waiting to shake her apart.

~

The photograph on my desk in the shoe factory is of a country road near Christchurch ripped apart on 4 September 2010 along the Darfield fault line.

The tree in the photograph appears to be completely unmoved by the event. It retains with its single-mindedness a sovereign sense of occupancy in a world torn apart.

The photographer's main interest, however, is in a small boy crouched by the violent crack in the road. It looks like a flesh wound made by a cutlass. The boy peers into the pits of the earth, while hanging onto his mother's skirt. A young woman with the pained look of a teacher burst in on a classroom of trouble has rolled the front wheel of her bike to the edge of the abyss. I have an idea she is a teacher—the way she leans over her handlebars looking for something that she already knows. The same cannot be said of the boy. He has just grasped the startling reality of a world rolled on, and paper thin.

~

It astonishes me that none of my siblings, myself included, ever asked the kind of questions that would open up our parents' past. But nothing much was offered to us.

In a beguiling way, however, nothing was actually something. It was an absence that encouraged an over-respect for our present circumstances and what we made of them. To remember went against the grain of progress, an attitude more commonly associated with pioneering forebears who juggled impulses to destroy with a need to create.

Christchurch sat on similar foundations. It too had grown out of a deliberate forgetting of what it sat on. Swamp. Peat. Trapped water. River gravels. And before the experts emerged to remind everyone that the top of the spire on the Anglican cathedral in the square had fallen three times to previous earthquakes, the idea that the city squatted over an area with a lively seismic history had been conveniently forgotten.

But water has a memory. This was one of the more devastating lessons from the earthquake, and was graphically illustrated on a YouTube clip. A man shovels a pile of more or less solid soil into a wheelbarrow. He picks up the handles and begins to wheel it over a bouncy cobbled drive, and within twenty seconds the grey sludge has turned to liquid.

This is what happened to the ground bearing the foundations of the city's buildings during the earthquake. In a few minutes a history of peat and swamp flooded a landscape thought to have drained its past.

~

We grew up unable to see much beyond the birth of our parents.

There was no big narrative to cling to, nor tales repeated from generation to generation until they acquire their own truth. The only story to come close was about my older brother Bob shooting himself in the foot after a night of rabbit shooting, an event repeatedly described as a tale of great mirth.

There might have been more to tell if more had been shared, if questions had been asked, if information had been offered and passed along at the moment it lit up in memory. But the family trait was silence. Great wreaths of it were wound around our lives and stuffed in the windows and hallway of our parents' house, and that is what was absorbed, that and, speaking for myself, a finely tuned ability to gauge the air in the room which at any moment might explode with the slam of a door. Someone had taken offence at something said—usually my mother. A seemingly innocent remark to her by someone commenting on the lousy weather had led her to say, 'Well, don't blame me. It's not my fault.' Now cups of tea would have to be ferried in and days of penance paid in silences that would not be broken until my mother's emergence from the bedroom.

It never occurred to me to ask my father if he remembered what his mother looked like, or if he had any memory at all of his father, or how many houses he lived in as a child. He did talk about his time on the goldfields, and I knew—without knowing how or why—that he was politically active in his thirties. And years later, when someone who had known him at the Wormald factory in Naenae said he was a 'shit stirrer', I was pleased to hear that, because it was not a side of him that I ever saw. I also heard that political meetings used to be held in our kitchen and that the Labour Party once asked Dad to stand in Hutt Central but he didn't because he could barely string two words together. Why? Nobody asked or offered a reason. It was just Dad, like the hills covered with gorse that packed in around our lives, a bit rough but capable of bloom. His ability with language improved after Bob's first wife, Ginny, a beautifully spoken part-Maori woman, gave Dad elocution lessons. By then, though, he was a man in his fifties.

I cannot hear his voice any more. I can hear my mother's, but only just, a whisper, her head held to one side, querying, suspicious that she is being got at. But Dad's voice has gone. A photograph is left to represent him. His eyes are round and motionless, like caves hollowed out by the wind. I cannot hear him speak, partly because there is always a cigarette in his mouth.

Often he is standing at the kitchen sink, staring out at the street. Mood and language moving about in their separate states. And this scene is often succeeded by another memory of him, in a bar in Kings Cross, Sydney. I am twelve or thirteen; we are on our way to Surfers, but first there is this night at the Cross to get through. And, more pressingly, there is this large thick-set American buttonholing Mum and Dad with his clean-shaven smell, his troubled eyes, and his desperation to win over my father. 'Do you understand how many troops we have over there in Nam?' His voice rising and tearing thin at the stupendous thing that he is about to share. 'Five hundred thousand.' My mother responds in her usual way, with disapproval, not at the information, but the intrusion, at the unwanted company. It isn't political engagement she fears, but engagement full stop. And, as well, there is the strong whisky breath of the man. She draws in her lips and looks away to lose herself in the smoke. A heavy man tucked inside a black suit smiled and sweated over a piano. The American leant forward to get my father's attention. 'Five hundred thousand men.' He sounded amazed by his own news.

~

Foundations come in all forms—texture, language, heritage, entitlement. Some things are buffed to be remembered while other things fall away. One world of upheaval gradually gave way to another. I saw not so much the things that remained standing but the gaps and fissures. Like the boy in the photograph, I found myself concentrating on a portal of memory that offered, at different moments, some incidents with startling detail and others that had been cast off but lingered defiantly, as if waiting to be hauled up from the abyss where all lost things lie.

One thing became clear. The sequencing employed by the basilica stonemasons was not available to me. Not all the bits and pieces had been accounted for. Nonetheless a picture began to emerge of the world as I had found it, as it does for an immigrant setting his eyes on the distant heads for the first time, before he sails through and ticks them off as known.

TWO

THE ROAD OUTSIDE the house at 20 Stellin Street, Lower Hutt, was my first horizon. The rubbish bins at the end of the drive were the heads I routinely stumbled out to each day in search of life.

Another new arrival—a kid of my own pre-school age—comes tottering towards me. He has broken out of the house across the road. A huge woman appears at the end of his drive. An enormous woman, her hair on fire, eyes big and wide. As soon she shouts the kid starts running on his short chubby legs. He is easily overtaken and carried back across the road. It'll be another year before he shows his face again.

At first my eye is drawn to those things that like me are a bit dumb, perhaps a bit vulnerable and witless, such as the dogs that lie on the road. Grudgingly they get up to let a car pass, then walk in a tight little circle before lying down again. For the moment the road marks the boundary of the known world.

I find myself waiting—endlessly—for something to happen.

Then I hear it. A screeching of brakes, followed by a terrible wailing. I wait—fighting back the mounting dread. Then I get out of bed, run down the hall and open the door in time to see a man carefully lift a sack over the hedge.

The last dog was run over as well, and its predecessor. But I know the solution. We will quickly buy a new dog, and give it the old dog's kennel and flea-ridden blanket and carry on as we were.

The first dog my parents bought for me was a little terrier the size of a handbag. I put it down my shirt and popped its head out over the top button so it could see the world approach. It was so excited, its little body shook and I felt the warm dribble of its piddle. It licked my face, it was so grateful to me for letting it piss over my belly.

One by one, my dogs are run over. There's hardly any traffic, and that is the problem. The event of a car isn't taken seriously, so the stupid tail-wagging fools stand up and glare at the approaching grille. In the World of the Dog the road belongs to them, a principle that they understand but nobody else does.

In 1960, I am aged five. It is a long wait until a car passes by. So from time to time I think to check on the deteriorating condition of the hedgehog. It was run over a few days earlier. There was more of it then. A black gummed thing. After a day it was half the size it had been. It was as though the air had gone out of it. Then it flattened out. Soon most of it was gone, licked up by tyres. The smell went too. There was a day of rain, and when I looked again the hedgehog was a light stain on the road.

Since then I don't like to look at it. In fact, I make a point not to look. At some stage in its slow evisceration I have become churlish. The state of the hedgehog has provoked in me feelings of disgust. So, if I don't look, it will be as if it isn't there. And, as I'd rather not feel the way I do when I look, then I won't.

In the course of making such choices I am slowly making me. But what are those choices based on? I could have found a stick and, while the hedgehog was still a moveable spiky ball, shifted the carcass into the gutter. But I didn't. I chose to look the other way, and that decision was perfectly in keeping with the climate of forgetting that will slowly infiltrate me.

—

In the long grass beneath the washing line I find an old boxing-glove. God knows how it got there. I look up at the sky. The leather's as hard as a sheep's turd at the end of summer. I have to push to get my hand inside, and I can feel it resisting me. Its last memory is of Bob's hand which is what it has moulded itself to, but in the end I win it over with my persistence, and then after I've done up the laces it begins to adjust until it feels as though it has only ever known my hand. The glove has a history—a violent, merciless one. I don't care about that. I'm just chuffed that it fits my hand. There is that initial awkwardness, but it soon passes. And I am left with the surprising and delightful feeling that room has been made for me.

~

My bedroom at 20 Stellin Street used to belong to my brother, but I cannot find a trace of him in there. He is seventeen years older than I am and has long left home. It's also hard to believe in what I have been told about Grandad, the bookseller, dying in there. I remember the hedgehog, and its slow fade from the road, and stare harder at the walls, at the ancient pinholes made from tacks and at the light patches where things used to hang.

When did I first become aware of my siblings? I suppose one day I looked up from my preoccupation with the carpet and there they were—legs, hurrying feet, their names, Pat, Bob, Barbara, Lorraine, and measurements dated and scored into the doorjamb of the washhouse.

On my way to bed each night I look up at a photograph taken of Pat, Bob and Barbara in a city street. They are young, as I have never seen them, and dressed in clothes that look to be from another era. The youngest in the photograph, Barbara, doesn't look much older than my five-year-old self. Lorraine has still to arrive in the world. I'm waiting in line behind her. What were they doing that day, and why was the photograph taken? There is another photo on the wall—of my brother peeping over two boxing gloves held like paws.

He doesn't live with us now. I have no idea where he lives.

He shows up for the Sunday roast then drives off, and is gone for the week.

But look at what he leaves around the telephone. Bits of notepaper with phone numbers scrawled on them and envelopes covered with sketches of boxers' feet set to different angles of attack and defence. The sketches are stranger now in recollection because of their disembodied effect—the laced boots, the beginnings of shins, and then the legs peter out. But I came to expect them and would look for them when he left because they were as predictable as dogs crapping on the lawns up and down the street.

Apparently all three sisters are beauties. I wouldn't have thought or known it. But boyfriends call endlessly on the telephone or surprise at the door. Whenever they do Dad sinks into his rows of cabbages at the back of the house. One sister given to panic hides under her bed whenever a certain guy shows up at the door. Then my mother will yell out to Dad to come inside the house and fish this one out. I have seen him do it. He has to get down on all fours and poke around with the broomstick. The same broomstick which he broke over my brother's back one night after a mealtime turned bad. Someone had said something.

And then, one by one, they leave. Pat, followed by Barbara, who will live in Rome and work as a typist for an American novelist, until there is just me and Lorraine at home.

Postcards from Ceylon and exotically named places arrive in the letterbox. I remember one from Alexandria, kids on it about my age in bare feet and pyjamas. The road looks dusty. Hardly a drop of concrete in sight. My father picks up the postcard in his thick armour-plated hands, dropping ash over it as he studies the picture, and shakes his head. I know what he is thinking. The poor little bastards without shoes, dressed in pyjamas.

~

Still, there are the regular and dependable sights. The letterbox. The steady hedge. And the strange sight of the mentally retarded boy from a house around the corner in Taita Drive eating our back fence until it was not so strange any more, but routine, along with the clouds and the trees and the crapping dogs.

Then one day there is an irregularity. The 'retard' has come to the front door. I can see his shadow through the glass at the end of the hall. This is completely and wildly out of the ordinary. I've only ever seen him eating the back fence and now, worryingly, he is at the front door. I hide behind the door at the top end of the hall and listen to Mum telling him in a firm voice to bugger off back home to his place. 'Go on. Off you go.' She never says that when he eats the fence, which we regard as normal, rather than this traumatic event of his turning up at the front door like this.

God knows, I love the bricks that our house is made of. They are the most beautiful pattern, and warm like a dog's coat in summer, a perfect companion for me and my ball, and dependable. When the wind blows, the house is immovable.

Bricks will stand by you. *Go on, blow, you bugger.* It is my father talking back at the windows. The story of the three little pigs still lies ahead of me, and when eventually I hear it, perched on a school mat, Dad's excited face will rush into my thoughts, startling me, and I will unwind myself from the floor amazed at this collision of worlds, and the teacher will twist around on her chair with the questioning look she usually saves for one of the kids who is always pissing himself.

The biggest and most influential factor in this life that I have arrived into is the Ministry of Works. I don't know that at the time, diverted as I am by the warmth of the footpaths and roads, which for all I know were here one thousand years ago. The Ministry of Works is in charge of dispensing concrete. There is another mad fool in Taita Drive—a shell-shocked ejaculator, who, like the redback spider, we have been warned to keep clear of. The Ministry of Works is more discriminatory about its flow than the shell-shocked man, who I learn is someone 'not in charge of his memory'. I've heard him mutter something which an older kid, who lives three houses down and who seems to know everything, says is Italian for an obscenity. You never know what the shell-shocked man will spray out next. Not so with the Ministry of Works. It pours concrete with endless and astonishing capacity, and the shape of the world gradually accrues over stamped down bracken and clay.

The MOW deity is honoured in a number of ways. Stellin Street, for example, is named after a city councillor. The primary school I attend is named after a minister of works, as is the street that winds around the school, lined with little state houses that scream out for a visitor.

The lack of occupancy, the constancy of the wind, the fabulous achievements of the Ministry of Works, and silence— all form the conditions of our daily existence.

It will be years before I hear the name of Ernst Plischke. And yet his fingerprints are all over my world. Plischke, an eminent Viennese architect who spent the war years employed by the Ministry of Housing, greatly influenced our interior space. He and his Jewish wife had come to the place on the planet furthest removed from upheaval in Europe and wasted no time in telling us what we had failed to see and appreciate for ourselves. Namely, we were awash in year-round light, so why not let that light inside our houses? Like a lot of good ideas it was immediately obvious. Our houses were shifted around to face north and the windows were enlarged to let the world into our lives. For the first time it was possible to stand at the threshold of our interior and exterior existence, to occupy two places at the same time. Mum could peel the spuds and look out the window to make sure I hadn't hung myself on the rope tied to the oak on the front lawn.

Eventually I get to leave the rubbish bins behind and wander up to the dairy at the top end of the street. A year or two later, when I am seven or eight, another graduation, and I am released further afield, to the Naenae Olympic Pool with my togs and towel tucked under my arm. I follow the railway tracks up Oxford Terrace and near the Naenae shopping centre duck down a piss-stinking subway beneath the tracks and rise to Plischke's vision based on the European square, which he had designed to encourage 'accidental encounter'.

Nowadays a Cash Converters occupies the shop where Dad bought me my first bike (second-hand, but newly painted). The picture theatre is now a medical centre and proudly displays a mural of the new community—faces from Ethiopia and Polynesia and Asia never seen or heard of in 1960, and tacked on the end is Plischke's own benign face. In the early 1960s he returned to Europe, disappointed with his ideas being watered down by interfering bureaucrats, disappointed by the lack of scale.

The space has since become even smaller, turned meaner. Graffiti has made its inevitable weary way here. The tower clock that had once seemed so majestic wants badly for majesty. A slap of white paint covers the building blocks. It does the job, which is all the Ministry of Works ever set out to do, and at the same time it infantilises and diminishes anyone older than nine.

The streets around the square are a spaghetti of switchbacks, right angles, gentle curves that keep on curving until a full circle is magically achieved, and dead ends that turn out not to be dead, unless you happen to be in a car. On foot, as nearly everyone was when these streets were designed, thoroughfares between the houses lead the way out. You may not know exactly where you are but once you understand that every street turns into another then you are never lost. You are simply on your way to somewhere. You may feel lost, but the feeling is temporary. The key is not to stop. Soon, everything will become clear.

~

The process of concreting has a dual purpose. As it disperses, the concrete emits through secondary and unidentifiable means a tremendous silence. And with that silence comes the kind of calm that only a forested valley left alone for thousands of years knows. This silence is deceptive, fraudulent. The concrete cannot keep everything down and sealed. Certain things leak out. Secrets. Clues pointing to small botanical tragedies. The magnolia with its rust-spotted flowers. The hedge that is so bright and green and alert to your thoughts, but then smells of decay in late summer.

It is a very quiet place that I have arrived at. Very quiet, and very still. The geraniums on the windowsill make you want to smile and forgive the quiet. Although when the silence cannot bear itself any longer the wind gets up. The leaves flutter in the air and drop into a new place. The trees do not normally rustle; the eaves under the tiled roof do not ordinarily whistle. But like a car starting up in the middle of the night, these disruptions pass and everything settles back into its astonishing silence.

I have seen trout lie still into the current. In the same way the world passes over me. Vast amounts of sky balloon by me, and this enormous silence.

Now and then a car passes and leaves a faint scent of petrol in the air. Perhaps next time the driver will wave.

Of the other signs of things having passed this way there is the worn carpet in the hall that my knees know well and the draining sound and smell of old dishwater. There are the usual companionable noises: the cardiac thump of the washing machine, the bossy and maniacal telephone that makes everyone jump. Since it is never for me I remain by the washing machine porthole watching a pair of circling pyjama bottoms. A large broad-shouldered fish floats by the window. It is the slipper I was wearing when I accidentally stepped on some dog shit.

At a neighbour's house I smell a sort of green that I cannot locate. It smells of shade and refinement. If I close my eyes and try hard I can just about retrieve it—or the sense of it, the surprise of it. Describing it is harder. I want to use the word 'tartan', but I am being lazy, and suspect I am attempting to introduce a known thing rather than the original experience which, as I say, alerted me to a trace of something that wasn't obviously present in the room. This green smelt of privilege. A Wolseley green. Deer. An antlered room. The shade I have mentioned. There was green up and down the street—on the front lawns, in the hedges and trees and even in the passing cars, and occasionally in a poor choice of clothing. But the trees especially—a gummy green that later I pick off my fingers. The green at our neighbours smelt both faraway and familiar. Or do I mean familiarly faraway? Whenever I visited the neighbours I smelt it, but only in their sitting room which was a 'glen' or a 'glade'. I'd seen both words on the labels of things.

A bottle, and something else, I forget what, but something quite unexpected. There was nothing like that particular green smell elsewhere in our lives. Later, on my way home from the Naenae Olympic Pool, as the heat went out of the day, I would catch the tarry grey smell released by the footpaths, and at some point I absorbed the idea that I had learnt to smell time.

Of the other smells of note: the cigarette-ash smell of my father passing in the hall or having sat in *that* chair, in *that* place and, above all, the smell of roasted meat—the air inside the kitchen bakes and sweats with it.

There are kitchen devices committed to the erasure of memory, such as the mincer, a beautiful and elaborate device. Pulling it apart and cleaning it of untraceable bits of animal and then sticking it back together is the highlight of doing the dishes. It clips onto the edge of the bench and grinds up the leftovers of animals that Mum turns into rissoles, very nice with a splash of tomato sauce. The world is constantly devolving and changing, and memory has to hurry to keep abreast. In the case of my parents, memory has long since given up the chase.

When I ask Dad what used to cover the hillsides before the gorse I wait for him to roll his smoke, and then light it and inhale. After the smoke funnels out of his mouth he decides he had better take a look at these hills, and briefly I have the feeling that I have just pointed out a feature of the landscape that wasn't there when he last looked, as though the hills popped up in the night. He gazes distantly, like he does at the beach. The hills. Yes. What used to cover them? He takes the smoke out of his mouth as if that might jog his memory. He looks all the harder. The hillside glows with triumphant yellowness, as though it wishes it could be even more yellow. Dad looks thoughtful—some useful information is on its way—but it turns out that he is simply mimicking someone deep in thought, or someone else's attempt to fetch a memory or dislodge a piece of information, because it turns out he doesn't know either.

Then he notices the rubbish bins. His face springs to. Why haven't I taken them in? *For Christsakes.* That's my job. To put out the rubbish bins when the lid is crammed down on newspaper packages bulging with animal remains, and then bring them in again when they are pleasingly and reassuringly light and easily picked up by their jug ears and swung along one in each hand. And then the pleasant ringing sound as the lid drops cleanly and evenly over the lingering smells of putrescence and foulness.

After the bins, I jump on my bike and track the seagulls on their route inland to the Wingate Tip where I climb over mountains of filth. The mud is thick, unhealthily rich. The smell of disinfectant catches in the throat.

None of this is visible from the street where Dad and I looked up at the yellow flowered hillside. Somehow one place is able to keep itself a secret from the other.

Machinery grinds away compressing everything, pushing the filth further and deeper into the landscape. It is hard to believe that the gorse could prosper, that a single flower could bloom out of this foul mulch.

There are paintings—at this time unknown, of course; but also I never suspected such a past to exist—of magnificent podocarp forest rising from the place of the tip, pushing over folds and bumps in the landscape and filling the valley floor. And, besides, I had never heard of the painter, or any painter for that matter, by the name of Samuel Charles Brees, who had once stood his easel where I stand at the tip looking down at the hideous mouthy grin of some unidentifiable animal gazing up out of layers of old newsprint and men's magazines.

~

At 20 Stellin Street little is known about anything except spot welding, knitting, rugby, and the right time to plant cabbages and put in the tomatoes. The residue of family lore is light. Some of it sticks. But it is like learning an isolated fact, such as Moscow being the capital of Russia. One grandfather was from Pembroke Dock. Mum's real father was a farmer, but we never hear his name spoken. Dad's mother died of hydatids. Mum's mother, Maud, 'the dreadful old bag'—I have absorbed that much—made a choice between her man, sometimes described as a leather merchant and a gardener, and her four-year-old daughter and gave Mum away. Some of it is hearsay, barely information, but a few words escape with a wipe of the mouth, something that wasn't meant to be said, and then a wave washes along the beach removing all trace of the footprints that I have been trying to wriggle my toes into.

At school when asked where I am from, I reply with the name of my street and the number on the letterbox. The teacher smiles. She adores me to pieces. I am so clever. Then I hear someone snigger, and I realise that I have given the wrong answer.

Something else was meant by the question. But thanks to Maud and the mysterious farmer and the drowned-at-sea man from Pembroke Dock and the one who died of hydatids, I have arrived into a potholed world.

~

But there are worlds within worlds, and the transition from one to the other can happen with remarkable ease.

From the worn carpet, we wander onto the ancient beach terraces that step down to the shoreline. A short car trip is required, but both places have the same meander and feeling of old occupancy and wear and tear.

Each beach terrace represents a separate upheaval. Years, millennia, crumble inside our shoes as we stumble and slide our way down to the water's edge.

Dad, with his fringe of bald man's hair, fumbles with his tobacco in the wind. Alone on the shingle he looks like the wind-blown stuff that catches on the thorny branches of shrubs that self-seed above the high-tide line, beneath the scooped-out eroded hillside that spooks my mother whenever she has to walk by it. They argue about this, of course. What is there to be afraid of? Dad only has to say that for her eyes to lift up to the overhanging cliff and for me to see that we will be engulfed by the hillside if we linger. He laughs and flicks his butt, then stops right at the most dangerous place to look back in the direction of the car. He's pretending he's forgotten something. Flaunting his fearlessness, while making fun of my mother's anxiety. It is hard to know which lesson to draw here—that the world is about to end, or that nothing will happen.

On the beach, he looks more alone than ever. He has spent fifteen years stuck inside train funnels with a welding torch, another twenty years getting up at the crack of dawn to walk to the Wormald factory in Naenae where he makes fire engines.

He is in his early fifties, perhaps five years younger than I am now, but already dog-tired. He has worked at physically demanding jobs since the age of twelve.

At the beach we move along the tide line like a family of mastodons, our heads bent and eyes lowered for whatever we can scavenge. We like things that are wholly themselves, and which can be taken without them losing value. Bits of pumice end up in the bathtub by the nail brush. The fish crate is turned into a useful weed bin. Cat's eyes by the tens of thousands are carried back in coal sacks and spread over the shingle drive.

On the way home we stop at the dairy and, digging in his pocket for his wallet, Dad retrieves rolls of fishing line which he dumps on the glass counter along with spare coins and old lottery tickets.

After a fruitless search of his pockets for his tobacco at a neighbour's house party he is briefly confused by the fishing line in his hand. Meanwhile, the woman with a tray of celery and cheese stands firm at the edge of the carpet, a boundary that I have been made aware of in a furious whisper—whatever I do, I must not stray across it with food in my hand.

The carpet is new, but the far bigger thing at stake is embarrassment—specifically, my mother's. She would rather avoid speaking to people than risk feeling embarrassed or inadequate. She would rather stay in the house than go out and risk judgment in the eyes of others. Sometimes I wonder why that is.

Down on the beach, she is completely at home and unguarded. I watch her pick her way through the kelp and driftwood and wonder if it is just parties she doesn't go in for—whatever the reason is. But I was right the first time. She is afraid—afraid of what others might think of her, and it never once occurs to me that this fear of hers has a history.

~

We are castaways at the beach, but also in the car. We drive for hours in order to live in a tent, in a place where there are others just like us living in tents, shitting in the same toilet, standing under the same shower heads.

As I am still young enough to go into the women's with Mum, at an early hour I am pulled from my warm sleeping bag and set down in the wet grass outside the tent.

Where are we? I have no idea. The sky, the trees and the

banks of grass are familiar and at the same time different, but different in such slight ways from those at home that I am not sufficiently interested to find out.

Indifference is the normal response to a campground where history is measured in rectangular outlines of dried trampled earth and perhaps a tent peg left behind, a sniff of domesticity clinging to the dead grass.

From out of the shadows the women appear—from various parts of the camp, around corners, from under trees, stumbling along in the dark in bare feet. In daylight they would cry out at sharp stones biting their feet, but at this hour, surrounded by the sleep of hundreds, their bodies go into a giant wince, and they resume their hobble towards the shower block. Mum and I toddle after them.

There's a light sitting inside a cage of steel mesh—that's interesting, perhaps the most interesting thing that I have seen in a day and a half. I stand there looking up at it, and then my wrist is grabbed and I am pulled inside the shed to join a long line among many lines.

A toilet flushes, and immediately all talk stops and our line takes a step closer. A young woman lifts a man's checked shirt over her head. I am amazed to see that she is naked. And because I look longer and harder than I did at the light inside the wire mesh I am aware of Mum's interest switching to me. I feel her hand land on top of my head and turn it like something left on the table to face the wrong way.

Older women such as my mother appear locked within

bodies stretched by pregnancy and scarred by operations, but others look like they were pegged up wet overnight and have just been taken down.

Under the showers they run a measuring glance over one another's bodies and stand with upturned faces as jets of water blast the night off them. Soon they emerge from the ablution block with pink glowing skins, in less of a hurry now, and speaking in noticeably louder voices.

From one municipal camp to the next we work our way across the North Island. There is always a ngaio pushing against the sides of the tent and and making scary shadows with its branches, and I seem forever to be standing in lines. I long for the moment we will pack up the car and head for home. I miss the street, the backyard, the slab of concrete and the brick side of the house where for hours I am content to throw a tennis ball and catch it within inches of the leaping dog and its snapping jaws. I miss the letterbox and the smell of the clipped hedge. I long for those certainties—even the sky which has its own particularity, shaped by the long gorsy hills that swallow and blow out tremendous gusts of wind. The settled air of elsewhere simply feels wrong, and when the moment comes to pull up pegs I am never so keen to help.

~

There are other journeys, of greater mystery. Blackbirds on powerlines and trees twitch through the windows of the car.

Where are we going? I have not been told, but I recognise something in my mother—her silence and resolute manner, tempered by something that I don't have the words for but years later will recognise as a helpless compulsion.

I can see all this from the back seat where I have been placed like a bag of groceries, expected to shut up and not say a word.

Dad is at work, making fire engines. He would be amazed to know that we are in the heart of Wellington in that rarely visited city, where 'officially' I have been only a few times, excluding these other occasions.

When we get *there*, we park. There is no suggestion that we should get out of the car.

From my place on the back seat I quietly shift to get the line of my mother's sight so I can see what she sees—a row of letterboxes, hedges, fences. I know the routine. We will sit in silence, unaware of ourselves or our strange purpose until a pedestrian walking by looks in the car window and Mum, hounded by the stranger's curiosity, makes a show of digging in her handbag for her face mirror.

I could ask what we are doing, but I don't. The question will not be welcome. The first time we sat there I could feel it in my bones. And, in any case, were I in any doubt, later, on the way home she says in a calculatedly casual voice that there is no reason for me to mention this little excursion to Dad.

The front door of a house opens. The quick shadow of someone dropping down a short flight of steps causes Mum's head to snap to. The person comes into view, but it is the wrong person, the wrong gate, wrong house.

Released from that tension we sit back, Mum's limp hands go back to the steering wheel, and we wait.

So, for what feels like hours, and perhaps is, we sit in the car and we wait for my mother to catch a glimpse of her mother, Maud, the woman who gave her away.

~

Out of the vanished or vanishing world of my childhood, figures come and go.

A girl, aged twelve, pregnant, her jersey pulled tightly over the hump in her stomach, is the most astonishing sight I have ever seen on the playing fields of Hutt Intermediate. At the sound of the school bell she remains there looking down at herself. The shadows of the other kids flee across the green fields. In her solitary world the girl continues to look at herself. She pats the ends of her jersey. She runs her hand down over her belly and when she looks up her face is filled with wonder.

Then one day she is gone. The grass where she stood is green and bristling. No one asks after her. No one says where she has gone. Instead, to the teacher's furious strumming on the ukulele, we bellow out a calypso song.

But how did that happen? A girl of twelve? No one asks, no one knows, no one thinks to ask. I wouldn't say that no one cares, but, like all the dogs that have been run over in the street outside our house and then forgotten, the pregnant girl has gone, and that is all there is to it.

Then, one night, on the other side of my bedroom door, the terrifying music of a television drama has waned, and in its place I hear tears and shouting, followed by the stampede of feet down the hall. The front door slams, and the house shakes. Car doors, one after the other, crack open and shut. A moment later, the car bursts off into the night.

I won't see my sister again for a while. Lorraine has gone to live with her boyfriend in a caravan. She has just turned seventeen and is pregnant.

Her bedroom used to be the one opposite the bathroom. When I poke my nose in there it still smells of her hairbrush.

On Sunday, we return to the beach to pick through the kelp thrown up by the storm that blew over during the week. The sun is out. It is a glorious day. My father's hair is whiter than ever. My mother hugs herself. Nothing was said in the car on the way here. Nothing is said about the pregnancy. The silence of course is occupied with nothing else.

I find a blowfish, perfectly whole in a way that other dead fish are not, as light as paper to hold, but when I look into its mouth and gullet I can find nothing there. It is completely hollow.

~

One day, the concrete layer is broken into and a huge tree trunk is unearthed at the end of the street by drainage workers. A crane and an earthmover have to combine forces and loop a chain around the log to lift it out of an ancient-smelling ditch. A crowd gathers and, to judge by the silence, it is in awe of this remnant from the erased world.

On another occasion an enormous slab of timber with the bulk of a Roman column is paraded through the streets on the back of a truck. We stop and stare as it travels by—massive, captured, like some barbarian of old paraded through Rome in chains.

No one knows its variety. The massive slab has been stripped of identity. It has moved beyond botanical association—beyond sympathy too for that matter, or a capacity to shock—to become building material.

After the ancient log was lowered onto the truck and taken away, the drainage workers leapt into the gaping hole and, stumbling over old roots, successfully joined the concrete pipes, and the sewerage line kicked into life again to pump its discharge out to the headlands where we like to walk at the weekend.

Thank God the ancient log has been disposed of. There is general agreement on this matter. Roots are hell to deal with.

Dad won't even have certain trees on the section. The 'show lawn' is covered with little notches, rips and tears where it has come under attack. In the afternoon heat, on all fours, hatchet in hand, Mum hovers and tracks the rooting system of a rogue plant that she never chose to have on the property and so it will have to be chased out. She slashes with the hatchet and Dad looks on approvingly. He is ready to crack open a beer, but won't until Mum is finished. He has been waging his own war out the back of the section. Rarely are they so close in agreement about anything. It has been drummed into me—there is no point in pulling out a weed unless you rip out all its roots as well.

The incinerator will smoke away into evening.

~

I have been born into a world of amnesia. And in the world of amnesia, language is first to go—talk of fairies and nymphs disappears the moment the shade they shelter in is destroyed forever by the rush of daylight across a forest floor as the giant trees crash to earth.

We tell ourselves that 'fairy' and 'nymph' are English words. We have no use for them out here in the new world, and so amnesia finds justification in false pride.

Before the MOW is able to coat the world in silence a forest must be cleared. The largest trees are scarfed to encourage them to fall in the desired direction. Starting with the largest trees of those highest on a hillside, a 'drive' is set up so that each one will crash and topple onto the next giant, which in turn cracks and drunkenly weaves before it too smashes down on the tree below. In this way an entire hillside falls like a stack of dominoes.

Then the fire lighters move through the fallen logs. The mayhem of men running like hoodlums with torches is captured in an 1857 sketch made by William Strutt. The fallen logs lie in a great tangle, like a battle scene described through the ages. It is chaotic, and pitiless.

The fires burn for days, and when the smoke clears the hills are covered in black stumps. The ground is black with soot.

For days the valley at the end of the harbour is lost in smoke. The sun disappears and, around sunset, turns into a fireball, which for the first settlers must have felt like a portent of the end of the world. The story of the hillside has been terminated. Gorse and grass take over, and a whole new story begins.

Smoke is the colour and texture of amnesia. Amnesia, like smoke, can only point to the condition. We are aware of a loss, not what it is that we have lost.

It is easier to dwell on the glories of what we have achieved. And, to show improvement, as in Charles Heaphy's 1841 watercolour of a land clearance. In the foreground, six tree stumps look like amputees but without engendering compassion. They don't shock in the way a log pulled out of the boggy depths by drainage workers does, because look at what has been won: a lovely croquet-smooth green field. In their supine and semi-stripped state the trees even manage to look elegant, almost improved upon. It would be easy to believe that they had signed their own death warrant for the sake of the greater good.

It is the end of a process that began with a makeshift plank bridging the gap between the decks of the *Resolution* and the primeval forest that William Hodges painted. Others follow, leaping off that plank with axes and fire.

Were it not for the likes of the naturalist William Swainson and the surveyors William Mein Smith and Samuel Brees, who compiled a painterly record of what they saw in our neighbourhood before it actually became one, there would be no lost landscape for us to imagine, let alone lament.

In one old painting is the riverbank where I played, but it is not as I found it. The still surface of the river holds the reflections of overhanging trees and bushes. A raupo hut occupies the near bank where, more than one hundred years later, the kid from across the street and I will sneak up on a car parked on the shingle, its windows steamed up. All we will see is a bare arse and a girl's startled face, before the car door is kicked open and a guy stumbles out pulling at his belt and swearing his head off. We tear into the scrub, most of it crappy undergrowth, bracken and gorse and broom, growing like weeds in place of the magnificent trees of the paintings.

Along with the original forest, the old Englishy names of the first homesteads—Algiony, Hawkshead and Herongate—thatched cottages that sat in a Garden of Eden, will disappear from collective memory. And the broad, many-fingered estuary of the river, which encouraged the first settlers to think of it as another Thames, will change its course.

In a sketch of his own place in the Hutt Valley, which he called Hawkshead, William Swainson delights in foregrounding introduced elements. Five bunches of English flowers shiver in the newly cleared space, forget-me-nots. The massive trunks of the forest push up through the top of the canvas in the background. Down by the river, a toetoe and a cabbage tree frame two cows drinking at the water's edge.

Soon enough Swainson is sketching men with long axes wading into the bush. Then the fires begin, the thick, sun-obliterating effect of the smoke follows, and amnesia sets in.

So it was easy to forget or, at least, accept grandparents and heritage as something that other people had, something that wasn't that interesting, or enviable, like owning a particular old artefact, a Victorian brooch or fob watch, for which there is no obvious contemporary use.

Years, decades, pass before I set eyes on Maud, my mother's mother, in Villa Rosa, a house on Bathpool Road in Taunton, Somerset. There she is in the album laid out on a table, photographed in the very same house that I happen to be visiting.

Mavis, a first cousin of my mother's (unearthed just a few years before my visit) will say of Maud only that she could be 'a hard woman'. Which isn't quite the condemnation I had hoped to hear. I wonder if Mavis picks up on this because she repeats, in minor key, 'She could be *very* tough.'

Well, yes, I should say so, in order to make the trade that she did, a trade my mother had no say in, and one that haunted her for the rest of her life.

As a matter of principle I grow up loathing Maud—at least the idea of her. Whenever asked about my ancestry, specifically my grandparents, I say with some relish, 'I don't have any.'

I never did see Maud in all of those times we parked in her street so Mum could catch a glimpse of her. This occasion in

Mavis's house is the first time that I have locked eyes on my grandmother.

She is not what I hoped for. But what did I hope for? I don't feel as though I have found another layer of me. She could be anyone. She has made no effort to smile for the camera. The eyes are flat, unyielding.

But then, in another photograph, her face has opened up to a generous smile and the transformation is staggering. She looks almost likeable. She has blonde hair. How strange. I wasn't expecting a grandmother with blonde hair. I check with Mavis. The photograph was taken on a visit to Taunton in 1922, eight years after my mother was born.

~

Briefly, Maud lived in the Hutt, in the same building where many years later, after a changeover from residence to a drapery and clothing store, Mum is buying me my first school uniform.

She is like a rooster in a familiar pen. Her eyes are everywhere but the task at hand. The poor woman across the counter is trying hard to get her attention. A decision has to be made. Should we go with the current measurement or carry on as we have up until now and allow for the inevitable growth?

This is how it will be for years to come—the lack of a natural fit, a looseness of material. I continue to grow, but it is a losing battle. I am forever too small. It will be years before neck and collar feel right together.

Perhaps my mother is experiencing something of the same in the drapery store. For when Maud lived here she sent for Mum, the little girl whom she had given up eight or nine years earlier, and my mother re-entered Maud's world. By this time Maud had had two more children, boys, Eric and Ken. No one knows why Maud sent for Mum, or what she had in mind. Or, for that matter, what my mother made of this re-entry. No one thought to ask. And, of course, Mum didn't say. But whatever the reason she came to live with Maud, it didn't work out, and for a second time my mother was given the flick. I believe she was fourteen or fifteen years old when this happened.

I wonder if this is what has my mother so preoccupied—squaring up this memory with the stacks of new-smelling school uniforms. As she opens her purse to pay she is still looking into that old space. But I know that the walls of a room do not remember a thing; they are the most hopeless of witnesses, infuriatingly discreet, dedicated as much to accommodating the new as they are to forgetting.

My mother's tragedy is that she cannot forget.

There is a photograph of Mum sitting in the sand dunes on Petone Beach, a little east of where William Swainson had once sat sketching the settlers' first thatched cottages nestled up to Te Puni's pā at Pito-one, which is now called Petone. Just back from the sand dunes today is the Settlers Museum. The prow of a sailing ship bursts out of its side. On the east side of the building, which faces the gorse-covered hills, is a stained-glass illustration of a settler carrying an axe on his shoulder, his wife, with a baby in her arms, and a boy who wades ahead of his parents into the bush, his eyes bulging with uncertainty at the adventure that lies ahead.

In the photograph, my mother, who must be in her mid-twenties, looks very thin and a bit troubled by the bundle at her side.

When my eldest sister, Pat, was born Mum must have hoped that Maud had softened a bit, that she might finally show some interest in her, and so, unannounced, she turns up at Maud's door to show off the baby—Maud's grandchild, her first, as it happens. Mum is kept waiting outside on the porch rocking the bundle in her arms until Maud returns to the door with a ten-shilling note in her hand and an instruction for Mum never to show her face again.

Then, some years later, when Lorraine's epilepsy is diagnosed and the doctor asks Mum if there is a family history, there is only one way to find out. This time Mum telephones Maud to ask the question that the doctor has asked of her.

'But,' says Maud, 'I have no daughter.'

~

Now, many years later, towards the end of her long life, my mother lies on a hospital bed staring dimly at the ceiling of the stroke ward in the Hutt Hospital.

I am required to help her fill out a form for the occupational therapist. To the absurd question, 'What is your life's ambition?', my ninety-year-old-mother suddenly rallies. Her eyes find mine. She is clear and unequivocal. Her ambition is to outlive Maud, who died in her ninety-fourth year.

Over the coming months, as she is whittled away by a series of strokes, and it becomes clear she won't achieve her 'life's ambition', we cram four birthdays—her ninety-first, ninety-second, ninety-third and fourth into the space of a few months.

She has to hold onto the rails of her chair as she draws in a mighty breath and leans forward and, with surprising gusto for a ninety-one-two-three-four-year-old, blows out the candles on the cake.

~

More than fifty years earlier she had given birth to me in this same hospital, but on a different floor, in a different ward, where the first joyful cries of life are heard every waking moment. The floor she is on now has the sly and silent air of process and procedure.

In the dark she seems unaware that I am sitting in the armchair in the corner of her room. She raises her hand from the bed to hold it above her and looks at it as if it is not part of her but something that in a bored moment she has found interesting. Eventually her hand flops back to her side, and her head turns to the pale light in the window.

Dawn. There will be another day after all.

I used to wonder if she ever wondered, *How strange to think*

I will soon be leaving this. Especially at night when the prospect of the end acquires its theatrical side.

For several weeks she has hovered in that twilight world, dumbly feeling her way along corridors that the dying are left to figure for themselves without information or guidance, bumbling along in a fog of morphine.

Half blind, she sniggered at the window. She fetched up the name of an old neighbour. And when I looked, a lumpy cloud was passing.

It is too late to ask her about Maud. It is too late to ask searching questions or to expect her to answer honestly of herself. It is too late for her to shed light on the past. On the other hand, the earthquake is still some years off and so I have still to arrive at the point where the past, in particular my own foundations, holds any interest. Maud, who knew so much, died many years earlier, unlamented as far as I am concerned, and now Mum is about to follow her.

I read to her, fragments from Chatwin's *In Patagonia*. I doubt she understood any of it, least of all that I was attempting to read life back into her. Sometimes she managed a show of concentration, as though listening—but then reading too felt wrong to me, or ill-chosen, absurd in a way, to use one's last days to concentrate on a writer's journey through communities of exiles in the wilds of a place she might not have known actually existed.

On the other hand, being read to returned some dignity to her—she was engaged, it seemed—and this was better than the crash bang of the breakfast trolleys and the patronising cheer of the nurses. This seemed to be the official approach: keep everything bubbling along to the end with a light humour.

When the doctor, a solid and charming older Indian man, arrived on his morning round, my mother's eyes lit up. She was almost girlish in her flirting.

Out of her earshot the doctor asked me, 'Has anyone told your mother that she is dying?'

The need to point this out to her hadn't occurred to me. Surely she knew. How could she not?

The doctor gave me a searching look. The warm regard of a moment ago disappeared. He took off his glasses and wearily examined them.

'So,' I said. 'Should I tell her?'

He looked up, found his smile, nodded, and after a friendly pat of my shoulder he continued on his round with a brood of junior doctors in their new white coats.

~

Her grey hair has fallen carelessly across her face. I smile, and she smiles back. She was about to say something. So I delay my 'news' and wait, even though it is months since she managed a sentence. She was last heard from when invited to state her life ambition.

Her eyes look up expectantly, and I realise I have got it wrong. She doesn't want to speak. She is expecting to hear something said. She turns her head on the pillow. She tilts her eyes to the door. She must have seen me talking to the doctor. So I bend over her and in the same bullying manner I have seen the nurses use, sinking her into shadow, I say, 'I thought I would get a cup of tea. Would you like one?'

The light returns to her eyes and she replies with a nod, and I burst out of there.

Outside her room, fake cheer rebounds along the walls—splashy paintings by school children. There is the rush of a female visitor's footsteps for the lifts, followed by the loud exuberance of a newly arrived visitor, a large, glowing fellow, his arms filled with flowers and crackling cellophane. That is what the flowers are—a replacement for words and the need to say what cannot be said. Others camp around the bed of a wizened family member. Some perch on the bed-end, numb with boredom. A hand reaches across a skeleton for the bowl with the fat bananas. Behind an open door a number of orderlies in green smocks have their feet up, eating out of chippie bags and laughing in gulps at an episode of *The Simpsons*.

I carry two styrofoam cups back to my mother's room, horribly aware of the length of the corridor, which shines with disinfectant and the sound of my own footsteps.

It is a moment before she is aware of me standing in the doorway. The old head turns on the pillow and smiles. I put down one cup, and hold the other to her mouth. She manages a sip, and shudders. I wonder if it is too hot. But that isn't it. I have forgotten she doesn't take sugar. What was I thinking?

I hurry out to make a fresh cup. By the time I return she is asleep, so I leave the tea on the cabinet by her bed and tiptoe away to the lifts.

~

The next day there is a photograph in the newspaper of a spectacular dying sun taken by *Voyager* on a journey to the outer reaches of the universe, in effect, to capture old news.

It is a snapshot of our own sun three to four billion years from now. A sun just like the one that provides our daily existence has imploded into vapour.

I bring the newspaper to the hospital. I show up to her door with one of my better smiles, one with firm and honest intentions. She is pleased to see me. The doctor has still to make his round. So I sit down on the edge of her bed with the newspaper open to the relevant section. I hold up the photograph of the dying sun. She leans forward, interested, and we go from there. And I continue to circle, ludicrously alluding to the solar system, imploding suns and so forth, until finally I have to say it. 'You're on your last legs, Mum.' It is like telling a child some horrible truth about the world. She looks up at me, concentrating on what I have just said. She seems interested, then annoyed. She turns her head away from me. But the insistent light in the window is no better. When she turns back, I am surprised to find her looking so cross.

'Are you angry?'

She nods.

'With what?'

And for the first time in weeks she actually speaks.

'With all of you,' she says.

'Of course,' I say quickly. 'It's entirely up to you. But you will need to eat.'

She reaches for the half-empty container of yoghurt that has sat untouched since breakfast on the arm of the dresser and with my help begins greedily shovelling spoonfuls into her mouth.

~

She died at home, and that morning the sun splashed against the end of her house, where she had spent so many hours sitting on the patio surrounded by plants, a cup of tea at her side, a pair of secateurs at her feet. The undertaker was over-dressed, and his ruffian offsider was also, grotesquely, in a black suit, but not quite as successfully turned out. Perhaps because of the rash on his face and the heavy black shoes, I thought of the boys' home I used to walk past. I would stop to look across the fenced ground and wonder about those boys my own age wandering in that state savannah, unloved as any dog at the pound. As I looked at the offsider's shoes and up to his face and back to his shoes, I wondered if he had come from there. Then I moved out of this slow tumble of thought because there were a number of practicalities to consider. Such as RIP. Mum's face was 'at rest' and 'in peace', and I was happy for her. I would have liked to wake her, were it possible, to pass on just how peaceful she looked in death. She'd have liked to hear. She always said I was too critical.

The older undertaker spoke in that special register that they must be coached in or pick up from the movies. For the moment we the gaping living, Pat and I (Bob and Barbara were making their way back from the US and Fiji), stood around the body. Did we want Mum to be carried out of the house head first or feet first? Such a question had never been asked of me. Years ago, when Mum moved to the townhouse across the road from the beach, she'd said spiritedly that the next time she moved it would be on a stretcher. But had she said 'head first' or 'feet first'? The undertaker and the apprentice directed their interest professionally to the harbour and the wheeling gulls. Head first, I decided. The undertaker breathed out, and I was assured that I had made the right decision. Then the apprentice breathed out as well, though a tad late, as I recall. The undertaker had another question. Would the deceased prefer to have her face covered or uncovered as she was carried down the outside steps? He said it was a matter of personal preference. Although, he said, the Greeks have a view on it. To which the apprentice nodded vaguely. Some prefer covered. Others uncovered. It's up to the individual. Well, clearly it was too late to ask Mum, so I decided on her behalf—uncovered. She should have the sun on her face this one last time.

We picked up the ends of the stretcher and shuffled towards the back door and got her down the tricky bit of the steps. Now it was just a case of sliding her into the back of the van. I'm sure it was a van, not a hearse. Mum wouldn't have cared. Or would she? It was too late for her to have an opinion.

I put down the stretcher and raised a hand in a silent command for the other two to halt for this last concession to my mother's lifelong love of the sun. And, as I recall, the sun lined up with the neighbour's roof and the rose heads nodding above the timber boundary fence and fell across her ancient face, which was jammed with deep lines but held only light- ness—neither bitterness nor disappointment, though she had known both in her long life. She hated feeling cold. She'd made my sister Barbara promise to make sure she went to the morgue with the cashmere shawl. And as soon as Barbara flew home she drove to the morgue with Mum's shawl. Then, as the doors closed, I did not think 'goodbye' in the usual sense or feel the sadness that comes with a parent moving out of one's life— although I would feel that later. Then, it was the shock that she would never again feel the sun on her.

~

Christchurch. Early morning. Steam rises off the fetid Avon River. At the Bridge of Remembrance the imperial gaze of the two lions recalls the female mannequin heads I'd seen at either side of the spotter's shed at Bottle Lake. Classical vanity on one side of town, the farcical at the other. And between these two poles the remaining bits of the city wavered.

Out at Bottle Lake, about ten kilometres north-east of the city, a large blowfly made me feel all the more aware of the ooze and smell of chemical heat, and the common end of all things.

The heavier rubble was being trucked out to Lyttelton Harbour and dumped to end up on the ocean floor near to, it occurred to me, the anchor marks of the first four ships that had carried the vision of Christchurch from one side of the world to the other.

A steady caravan of trucks dumping lighter material operated six days a week through the winter at Bottle Lake. A pile was growing by two thousand tonnes a day. Sunday afternoons, the trucks took a break, and that was the best time to visit. Without their grinding noise the silence was stunning and had physical presence, and something else that was uncomfortable to bear, like the weighty silence in a room where no one can quite bring themselves to remark on some stupendous event that has occurred.

A light easterly pushed the brush and sweep of the tide through a screen of pine trees. The trees didn't look quite right either. It was as if they too were in on the secret, and I was reminded of those grassed areas in Europe covering up places of old atrocity. There always seemed to be a fringe of pine looking on, as this one at Bottle Lake did. Twenty years ago, the tree-planter kept turning up limbs of dolls which, I'm told, had fallen a century earlier from the careless hands of children perched on the city's old shitter boxes which were cleared once a week by the nightwatchman and carted out to the Burwood refuse pits where Bottle Lake is now.

For several hours I wandered the edge of the mountain of debris as I used to comb the shoreline with Mum and Dad, picking up things, kicking the cruddier stuff away with the toe of my shoe. I never realised how much of a city is made up of junk.

Much of what I found had given up all allegiance to its original form, and it was near impossible to tell personal and public apart, so intertwined had they become. A golf club, a ski boot, a sales sheet with advice on how to deal with a negative response, a surprising number of old car manuals, books, lengths of timber, cracked and split, bricks, some masonry, sheet iron, and there a yellow bathtub duck—all found a collegial relation-ship that they never knew in their former lives. Shoes by the score but never a pair, hand-written ledgers in smart blue ink for amounts in the old currency that must have sat in an unopened drawer for the past fifty years.

And what I felt, above all, was a compression, that time itself had been compacted, and that the tip offered itself as a register of breaths taken, a whole century of breaths taken in rooms that no longer existed. By simply lifting the sodden layers you might find a breath taken a week ago, or in 1949, or 1892, when the first man in Christchurch to have read Samuel Butler's *Erewhon* (an anagram of Nowhere) stopped breathing.

I came to a pile of books leaking out of the side of the debris. I opened one and found it was from the city library. I turned two or three others over with the toe of my boot as though touching a carcass. Then I saw a red cased hardback and bent down to retrieve from the muck a weathered copy of Pliny's letters, and, as these things sometimes happen, the pages opened to where Pliny the Younger begins his letter with a description of the death of his uncle during the eruption of Mount Vesuvius. One line seemed so pertinent to my own exploration that I wrote it down: 'a letter is one thing, a history another, it is one thing to be writing to a friend, another to be writing to the public.'

—

The letter begins with a description of the afternoon before Pliny the Elder's death.

Pliny, the historian, who is in his mid-fifties, has taken a stroll in the sun, enjoyed a light lunch, and retired to his study, when he is called outside to observe a strange cloud 'bright with cinders' rising in the sky. Curious and wanting to take a closer look, Pliny makes arrangements for a light vessel to be prepared. He is about to get on his way when word arrives from the wife of an old friend asking to be rescued from their villa at the foot of Vesuvius. The plan to observe a spectacle is now a rescue mission, and Pliny orders a larger vessel to be made ready for departure.

Pliny the Younger chooses to stay back, and so from this point on the written account relies on the word of others.

In another important shift, the volcanic display becomes

merely a theatrical backdrop to the bigger and more urgent matter of Pliny the Elder's death, thus combining public catastrophe with an opportunity for family myth-making.

There are a number of heroic stages. One is Pliny's decision to remain on deck and brave the cinders and burning black rocks that shower down onto the galley. It is this casual courting of danger that the nephew is so keen to pass on. In addition to the burning sky, an out-going tide threatens to strand them before a favourable wind delivers the ship to Stabiae, the next heroic stage, where Pliny finds his friend Pomponianus in an agitated state. Pliny adopts a light spirit in an attempt to soothe his friend's nerves. After a wash he sits down to a meal in a cheerful mood.

As the eruptions grow more intense, Pliny assures his friend that the people have already abandoned the villages that are in flames. He then retires, dropping into a 'sonorous sleep'. During the night the entrance to his sleeping quarters fills with ash and falling stones. Before the escape route is entirely blocked by falling debris Pliny is woken by his slaves—seeing the danger he rallies the others. Pomponianus is too frightened to leave his bed, so the others, led by Pliny, debate whether to stay in the house, which is now rocking from side to side, or to flee for the open.

They decide on the latter and tie pillows to their heads for protection against 'the storm of stones'. It is morning, but because of the freakishness of the eruption it is as dark as night.

So far the letter has concentrated on describing Pliny's

sanguine mood rather than his appearance or condition. There has been no indication of a man struggling with himself or with the fumes from the eruption, but when he arrives at the shore he lies down on sail cloth and asks for water. Two servants are required to help him to his feet, but unable to support himself Pliny the Elder immediately collapses and is abandoned.

Three days later, a rescue party returns to find the famous historian buried beneath a layer of pumice.

~

Pliny the Younger's account is a letter addressed to the future. I thought of writing something in the same spirit. At the moment of retrieving the book from the tip face, I was beginning to rake over traces of a past, or at least to think of a past, however slight. I did not wish to disqualify a damp imprint left behind on a coloured tile at the Naenae Olympic Pool. Or a recitation of the names of all the dogs run over by cars arriving suddenly and catastrophically some time in the early 1960s on the road outside the house at 20 Stellin Street. But in thinking about these things I realised I knew the lineage of my dogs better than my own. The chances dogs took to uphold their own dignity in a world ruled by cars would introduce me to grieving. My job raking up the leaves spoke of another passing, as did the cool draught around my ears after a hair cut. But hair will grow back, and the leaves will go up in a puff of smoke in the incinerator, and the grass will spring back in the dead patches where the leaves have lain too long, and one dog will replace another, and each dog name will be more exotic than the last as if an echo of a faraway place will save it.

Such events are not compatible with the act of remembering. And in the concrete domain of this world nearly all the echoes I hear are of my own making.

The *Australasian Post* is a highlight of my visit to the barber. Especially the illustration of the pub in the outback, which is the first thing I turn to. Look at all those corks dangling from the brim of the swaggie's hat. I can see them clearly but not once do I connect them with the flies. I have to be told. In fact, as I recall, there were no flies until I was told about the job that the corks do. After that I saw flies everywhere in the picture. Just as no one ever suggested, and certainly I never dreamt as much, that beneath these foundations of hair oil and chit chat had once stood Wi Tako's house Te Mako. Or that fingers of estuarial waterways were once filled with eel traps. Wi Tako was an ally of the local chief Te Puni, whose people had helped the settlers ashore at Petone Beach. It never occurred to me that the kids I played with at school were descendants of a scene reconstructed in a painting. Emigrant ships are moored out from the beach. The castaways have made landfall at last, and local Maori are carrying them and their things to shore. I just thought everyone had come down in the last rain.

The concrete has done a grand job of covering everything up, yet the history is still there if you know what to connect to its smell.

Between sneaking up on cars parked on the river shingle we slip away to a piece of land that has no equivalent elsewhere in our lives. The smell is damp and boggy. Our 'pre-historic' scene is an old botanical battleground which the willows won, then lost. Huge trunks have been cast out of the ground to lie every which way. Some of the unearthed ones continue to grow, as though they have not been told of their fate or have chosen to carry on in spite of it, like a chicken that continues to run on because it always has, despite the fact that its stunned head lies on the chopping block.

What we can smell is the swamp our forebears turned the forest into by cutting down the trees. In heavy rains the river flooded and proceeded to cart banks of soil out to the river mouth, and beyond, so that by the time I have come along the original sea floor lies beneath two metres of mud. The smell of the willow is the stench of an old mistake. Of course we don't know that. And even the exhilarating sight that spring of the golf course in flood, turned into a disc of silvery water and shimmering with the shadows of windbreaks and cypress trees, fails to alert me to the rash actions of the past. The willows were planted as a rearguard action to hold the world together. And the timbers sticking out of the riverbank are the remains of groynes built by settlers in an attempt to correct their mistake.

~

In May 2011, three months after the February earthquake, and one month before the follow-up shake in June that deflated hopes of the city's quick rebuild, I went searching for the cinders of my past. I entertained a hope that, like the flies in the *Australasian Post*, all I had to do was identify the unacknowledged events of the past and history would flare into visibility.

I thought I would begin with a trip to Pembroke Dock in Wales, to visit the birthplace of my father's father, 'the man who drowned at sea'.

THREE

I REMEMBER THE smell—that whiff of familiarity you get when slipping on an old shirt. In this case it was the smell of old takeaways, which I always associate with England. I barely remember the face. But I remember his eyes. They were dull, mackerel. A chirpy mouth which for some reason made me think of the *Daily Mail*. Face like a schoolboy's. I imagine he was pushing seventy. A former jockey, perhaps, unless he was sitting down. I couldn't properly tell because the cashier's window separated us and I had to stoop to deliver my request through a small mouse hole in the bottom of the partition. His mackerel eyes slowly found me. 'Pembroke Dock,' he said. 'You're going to a place that used to be a place.'

I wished for something equally witty to say back. There was a pause from the other side of the grill, as if he, too, expected it. But instead of words came a jumble of images. I saw again the face of the young TV reporter and the lurch of the camera so that the wall of a building turned into a longer view of road, which, in the railway station on the other side of the world, threw me off balance, and when I looked down I could see the whiskered mouth of the cashier through the hole in the corner of the grill. But I had nothing to give back, nothing useful to say.

On the train, I was hostage to a solitary voice holding court at my end of the carriage. An overweight young man stood in the aisle hovering over his mates: one a short wiry figure who sat ramrod upright like a corporal silently absorbing a sergeant's hectoring, the other a tall lugubrious fellow who kept escaping to the view in the window. Golf courses were mentioned, too many pubs to remember.

Surely there are better things to recall, but all this time later after the names of the courses and pubs have melted away, along with the sullen victimised expressions of his prospective golfing mates, pitifully, it is the embarrassing pride I felt at hearing 'New Zealand' come up in the monologue. It came as the fat man mentioned the earnings of Tiger Woods' caddy, and I thought, what a strange connection to make with a country that had just suffered a major earthquake.

Surely this event was the one on everyone's mind? But no, it was not. What was on the mind of the little girl in front of me was the unopened bag of crisps in her mother's hands. What preoccupied the mates of the golf bore was how they might dodge the proposed holiday.

I looked out the window—paddocks, trees, the backs of water-stained houses. Down at my feet was another England. A newspaper with the print of someone's heel. Rooney's grimace as he turns from the goal mouth with his fist held high. I opened a book, but I couldn't make sense of the words. I found myself drifting back to a different world. I saw the night-lit streets of Christchurch and rescue workers in bright-coloured vests. I gazed out at the world sliding by the carriage window. I was on my way to a place that used to be a place. I looked out the window, and for a moment or two it was possible to identify a tree before it swept by, and then my thoughts returned to the landscape of upheaval.

With the critical unwavering eye of the self-portraitist I saw myself back on the couch at the shoe factory, staring at the television. I thought about Mum, although not so much the person or even her face, but the word itself. Spared of any helpful context it sort of cartwheeled across mental space I had cleared with the observation of the tree in the carriage window.

I thought about Wales; one of the managers of the operation at Bottle Lake had a Welsh name, and when I asked him about it he confirmed that his father had played rugby for Wales. We had driven to a different part of the dump, to a grey desert where silt from the liquefaction had been trucked and abandoned in vast quantities, which created a landscape like no other—grey, sinister, casting deep shadows. We sat in the car surrounded by a vomited up subterranean past, and spoke of places in Wales neither one of us had been. I mentioned Pembroke Dock. I even used the word 'grandfather'.

'And, do you feel yourself to be Welsh?'

Twice I have been asked that question. The first time was at a rugby match. I was startled to be asked. I was fourteen years old, and after the Welsh Dragons' demolition of Wellington at Athletic Park, I slipped into the Welsh supporters' end of the stand, drawn by their colourful scarves and singing. I must have given an answer that pleased because I arrived home draped in scarves and covered in pins and badges. Looking back, I think this is how each new Dalai Lama must feel. One moment he is playing with his toys and in the next looking up at a courtly circle of inquiring faces. It was the strangest thing, but it really was as though I had been found. For a moment I was Welsh.

The second time I was asked, I replied, 'I might feel Welsh if I knew what it feels to be Welsh.' Silence. My interlocutor, a man older than myself, adjusted his face as if to accommodate some sudden movement of mine. But I hadn't moved awkwardly or evasively. I had spoken confidently and, I thought, with some humour. I probably felt pleased with myself on account of this repartee, which is quite uncharacteristic of me, perhaps even a bit Welsh. But the man, who might have been a High Court judge or a fisherman in a previous life, continued to regard me in silence as though I was a curiosity, a piece in the museum, familiarly in other words but, at the same time, as someone who had fallen so far away from his source that he didn't know as much for himself.

And now I was on my way to Pembroke Dock. Beautiful

coastline, the cashier back at the station told me, popular with hikers. But I wasn't going there for either of those things. I was going there precisely because of what it used to be but no longer is.

—

The gappy shadows that had hung about over Wiltshire all morning shifted, and Trowbridge where I'd spent the night was overtaken by fields which never really got started before turning into something else, which then lost heart in its own endeavour and reverted to fields. Now and then a canal boat appeared stuck in a narrow stretch of dark water, and in comparison I felt as though I was definitely on my way to somewhere.

I was saving my eyes for Wales. So while there remained this bit of England to get through I shut them. I must have dozed off. When I woke it was raining. The golf bore and his mates had got off somewhere, and the little girl had won the war over the bag of crisps. We were stopped at a station. I sat up and looked out. I was in Newport, Wales.

Then we were going again. Wales moved by in the window. Old sky, old stone walls. Here, the rubble held together and the old was allowed to stagger on. Houses the colour of pumice tilted down the hill towards the railway tracks. Sheep. Sky. Grass. Great swathes of unoccupied space but, like the telltale bare patches of the campgrounds we used to pitch our tent on, there were signs of older occupation, of a landscape shaped and moulded, then abandoned and allowed to spring back almost to what it once was. I thought it was much like home, which is why it required such an effort to look again, to look carefully at the three men standing in a paddock, one leaning on a shovel. The three heads inclined to one another in complete agreement with what one of them has just said.

One man in particular caught my eye. I watched him slide by in the carriage window—a bit of shoulder heft, gentle face— and in a split-second my father has gone.

He is as I last saw him, in 1975, in his coffin, an angry bluish face. Not really him at all, but some poorly rendered version—a face blinking out of quartz, always perplexed—which is the version that endures in place of the jolly bloke with a glass in hand. There he lay, a man I never saw ride a bike. A man without language. A face often red with unexpressed anger. The day has ended inconveniently. Not at all how he expected. Just that morning he'd kicked the wheels on a new car and taken the cap off the radiator to sniff the water. That afternoon he lay dead on the floor of the bathroom at home.

The undertakers have been and gone, and taken Dad with them. Still, it is hard to believe that he won't walk in the door any minute. So until he does we sit grouped around Mum in the living room eating fish and chips out of the paper on the floor.

But of course Dad doesn't return, and later that evening I drive back to my student flat in the city in the new silver Mitsubishi Galant that he had been so eager to show off. Out of breath with excitement, I heard. The last word he managed to get out was 'Joyce'. But the footsteps running up the stairs were not those of my mother, but my brother's girlfriend, Renee.

Now I'm driving the Mitsi into town. It seems to drive well. Dad's black onyx ring is on my finger. The undertakers had taken it off and given to Bob, who gave it to me, which was nice of him, thoughtful in a way I didn't properly register at the time. In the back seat are a number of Dad's socks and a suede jacket. I don't know why Mum thought to give them to me or why it had had to happen just then. I didn't like to say 'no thanks'. The socks are a bit worn and a bit small but I will wear them through the winter until toe and heel have disintegrated. I will never wear the suede jacket, but I'll haul it from one flat to another.

A few days later I stood before his open wardrobe. A neat row of shirts seemed to be waiting for him to return, and I thought his death was probably a trick. It's what his row of shirts believed, and so I found myself suspending judgment. He will step out from behind the shirts and surprise me. And his jokey smile will emerge as it used to from the incinerator smoke while I pawed the earth around the cabbages. Meanwhile, the wardrobe stirs with his smells—cigarette ash, Old Spice, his beloved shoe nugget.

Fish is what I thought of—it must have been the rack of shirts—the herrings we used to catch and line up on the shingle like prizes, their silvery iridescence setting fast like paint, and how much I hated to rip the hook from their mouths.

The year before Dad died I was nineteen and living at home,

and Lorraine's father-in-law, Gordon, rang the house. He asked if Dad was there. I told him no. 'Well, what about Joyce?' I said, 'Mum isn't here either.' I heard him draw a breath. He said, 'I've got some very bad news. Lorraine is dead.'

What did I say to Gordon? I don't remember. No one had ever said a thing of such enormous gravity to me. I've got some very bad news, he said. After I put the phone down, my only thought was to tell Dad. It was late on a Friday afternoon so I knew where he would be. I got into the car Bob had lent me and drove there. The shadows had spread across the bowling green. The members were upstairs in the clubhouse bar. As I climbed the outside wooden steps I could hear the happy voices. They seemed so distant and apart from the news I brought. I stood in the door and, without anyone pointing me out or whispering in his ear, my father turned from the bar, surprised to find me. I'd never climbed those steps before. Then he dropped his eyes—he was always a stickler for club rules—annoyed to find me in jeans and bare feet.

I walked up to him and simply passed on what Gordon had said: 'I've got some bad news. Lorraine is dead.' It remains one of those moments I would like back. So that I might do it better. I wish I could have told him in a more careful manner. I wish I had done it so much better. But I was nineteen and all that goes with being that age. On my way to the bowling club I hadn't bothered to think about *how* I would tell him. The important thing was to pass on the information, the *terrible news*. And I had done so with the same grace as passing on a fish-and-chips order.

I can imagine the terrible shock he must have felt. I don't remember what he said—I had hardly given him the chance to absorb or to feel anything. I was impatient to get him out of there. His face turned red. He became agitated, as though he couldn't find the right thing to feel or do. His hand dived into his pocket for his keys and he quickly followed me out. He insisted I leave Bob's car and drive with him. He drove, badly and erratically, graunching the gears. It was as though he had forgotten how to drive. As we took the bend at Windy Point the front wheel hit the kerb. He pulled the wheel back and crunched down a gear, then muscled it back with the same brutal disregard.

Lorraine had been out the night before, partying. She woke early with a fit and choked on her vomit.

Mum was a few hours' drive away, visiting my sister Barbara in the Wairarapa. Dad must have telephoned her. I have no idea what shape Mum's grief took. It wasn't shown, at least not to me. She turned inwards, went down deep to that place where she'd been many times before whenever the world needed to be blocked out.

We drove to Auckland in separate cars. Mum with Barbara. Dad, Barbara's husband and I in the other car. At Lorraine's house, Dad sat on a low window seat, covering his face and shaking his head. I heard him say he would gladly swap places with Lorraine. At the crematorium I sat beside him, and as the curtains closed around the coffin a sob more wretched than anything I had ever heard escaped him. Then came the dreadful mechanical sound of the coffin descending to the furnace, and Dad half stood beside me.

A year later he was dead.

Dad's surviving siblings came to the funeral. That is, the ones who had remained in touch in the years after they left the orphanage. But where was Arthur? In Canada, someone said. In jail, someone else thought. Or maybe he was dead, as I tend to think, although no one said so. What about Laura? I didn't hear her mentioned. Jack was there, hard to miss Jack, no teeth, gummy smile, his eyes glinting with mischief. Jack's twin Gladys came. So did Percy. He was a taller version of Dad, amiable features, reserved. He wore a grey vest beneath his suit. I thought he looked like a man from another century. Or a solicitor. Although by reputation I only knew him as a drinker at the Kiwi pub in Auckland. While briefly attending Auckland University I would pass the Kiwi, and slow down and think, maybe I should go in and say hello to Uncle Percy. But the idea of an uncle, like a grandparent, seemed a bit far-fetched, and besides, what would we say to each other? Percy died a year after Dad, and his son Alan sprinkled his ashes over the Alexander Raceway. Years later I stopped outside a pub at Bulls to see Jack. I had driven up to Auckland to pick up Jo, my newly-wed, who had flown in from the States the day before. We were driving down through the island and I was eager to show the country off to her. At Bulls I had the idea that we should stop in and see Jack. Jo had never met anyone from my family.

Dad's funeral was the last I had seen of Jack. He had since

retired and now spent most of his time at the pub where in return for clearing the glasses he drew free beers. I looked around for his face. I couldn't see anyone who looked like Jack. I asked at the bar and an old shuffling fellow with his back turned was pointed out to me. I walked past the pool table and tapped him on the shoulder. He turned slowly—it was Jack, more dazed than I remembered. He looked up at me without any recognition. I had to mention Dad, and then his eyes lit up. He didn't have his teeth in that day, and I couldn't understand a word he said. He wasn't drunk. But without teeth and after a few beers Jack was incomprehensible.

Jo, however, held up her end brilliantly. She seemed to enter into actual conversation. Jack was beaming and my wife was smiling in her American way. I thought she was pretending to understand Jack, but later she told me that half the trick was to get onto the same wavelength, something she had remembered from studying Spanish.

From a child's point of view, Jack was easy to like. He was excitable, always on the brink of laughter. The world was best sampled with a beer at your elbow.

In the general exhibition called 'Jack' I have a crinkled photograph taken at the Pyramids. In the foreground a group of cheerful faces peer out from under lemon squeezer hats. One of them is Jack—at least, I think it is. I can't be absolutely sure. I have a sneaking suspicion I may have requisitioned the photo from someone else's album and inserted Jack. But he did serve in Egypt, and on his return he was given a serviceman's farm.

I have a very distant memory as a child visiting a farm. It is a fiercely hot summer's day, there are horses, a bare hilltop on a northwest lie. The farm, I recall, was a few hours' drive north of Stellin Street. I wonder if it was Jack's farm. One other scrap of memory insists Jack had a butcher shop, but it went broke. Too generous for his own good; always giving away meat. Gregarious in that way that Mum disapproved of in Dad. Jack insisted on stopping at every pub up the line after Dad's funeral. A beer for every year of Dad's life. I think that was the idea. But I wonder how much they knew of each other's lives.

~

On my way back into the old centre of town in Trowbridge I had found myself in a dingier world of cold shadows, cooking fat smells, and young sullen parents pushing prams ahead of themselves like figures from an accursed race. I wanted the sunshine back and so took a street in the direction of the green and golden Wiltshire countryside I'd seen from the window of my room.

In a quiet street across the road from the old church, I stopped to look at a stuffed pike on display outside the window of a secondhand dealer. What actually caught my eye was the inscription: *Caught by E. Laver 1909, wt 21lbs*. The year—1909—rather than the pike, or the pike and then the year.

I've always relied on 1909, the year of Dad's birth, as a way of securing the past, which, at that particular moment, in the best possible spirit of discovery, happened to include the champion pike.

I was aware of someone watching me from the sunny church wall. A moment later the shop proprietor pushed off the wall and ambled across the road to join me. I looked up with a nod, and he replied with the same. Setting his hands on his hips, he stared at the pike.

For some time we stared at the pike together. I was on the brink of telling him that in the same year as my father was pulled from his mother's womb the pike was dragged up from the deep ponds of Bowater, when the proprietor piped up. For years, he said, the pike had been on display in the tackle shop around the corner. Then, after the shop ran into financial difficulties, he had offered to take the pike off its hands.

'It is a big pike,' I said, and then wondered if I was right— by pike standards—since I knew nothing about them. The man said he had once seen an eighty-year-old pike. He held out his hands, and calculated the one on display to have been around thirty years old when caught. He imparted this information in an amiable manner, and then he said, 'Four hundred quid.'

The shock of the price sat between us. It jarred the air. Impossible not to notice, and perhaps the proprietor did, because a moment later, from behind his hand, in a more humble tone, he said, 'A bit less, if cash is involved.'

As I felt no need to comment or commit, we went on staring at the pike.

'It really is an attractive specimen,' said the trader.

Yes, I thought, but what would I do with it? I like to travel light, and the next day I would not be setting off to Pembroke Dock with a twenty-one-pound pike in the overhead luggage rack just because it happened to share a birthday with my father.

As the air between us turned mercantile the trader shifted beside me. There wasn't yet a froth of desperation, but I could feel it on its way as he searched inside himself for more pike knowledge.

Pike have a flat mouth. In this specimen the teeth were sharp and evenly spaced. But its eyes, I noticed, weren't right. More like a possum's or a rabbit's than a fish's, I thought, or for that matter, like the hazel-coloured eye of an owl.

The trader confirmed that the pike's eyes weren't its own.

'Eyes generally disintegrate,' he said.

I didn't know that, and said so.

'Everyone's eyes disintegrate,' he said. He used to have several boxes filled with false eyes. He had them by the hundred, in yellow and blue. 'Whatever you fancy,' he said. Perhaps he still had a box of eyeballs lying around at the back of the shop... if I was interested?

I hate to disappoint, a trait I suspect crafted by the past, but I didn't want him searching for eyeballs which, no doubt, after much huffing and puffing I would be obliged to examine and perhaps even buy. I told him not to bother, as he suddenly remembered where in the shop he had the stash of eyes.

'No,' I said, and it came out more emphatically than intended.

He looked a bit hurt.

'Please,' I said. That's what I meant. Then I thought to ask what he knew about the angler E. Laver.

'Nothing at all,' he said, but he could recommend a trip to Bowood, a lovely estate ten miles further up the road. Then he proceeded to tell me what I could expect to find there—the dark ponds, one of which the pike had come from—and after he had described the contents of the exhibition room, which I was surprised to hear includes Napoleon's death mask and a selection of his handkerchiefs, I felt no need to go.

~

I had to switch trains at Cardiff, and on the platform I picked up a certain register of voice that brought my father roaring back to life. At a neighbour's party he is speaking too freely, too enthusiastically. I can tell from my mother's frozen expression at the light dancing in Dad's eyes. And there it is, captured within the same frame, two different responses to rejection and abandonment. In my mother's case, a life-long fear of being judged unfavourably, and in Dad's a ready sociability that carries him from campground to campground across the North Island, an ability and willingness to make friends in situations temporary by design, in a rugby crowd, say, and certainly at the pub. With a few drinks under his belt that campground banter of his worked, up to a point.

But I have no idea of the country that sat inside my father.

There were so few despatches he shared.

I remember the day I caught him at the piano. It was a new piece of furniture in the house. When I was ten or eleven there had been a change of circumstances—a stunning reversal of fortune.

A vase of flowers sat on the table, a painting on the wall, a Parisian street scene by Raoul Dufy. I have no idea how it got there. The promise of performance extended to Dad—there he sat at the piano, his face straining to hear whatever notes he heard in his head. It was such a surprise, so unorthodox, like coming upon a dog preparing to mount a bicycle and pedal off under its own steam. He didn't know I was there. If he did he would have sprung up and coughed his way out of the room. While I stood in the door, I hardly heard him produce a sound. Was the room was too well lit? The gloom favoured by day-time drunks would have suited him better, rather than this hard, unforgiving light pouring through the windows. His hands spread lightly over the piano keys but no sound came out. The piano assumed complete control, as though it had a wire around my father's throat.

I drifted away, wishing I hadn't seen what I had seen. I would rather have known that he couldn't play the piano—which would have been no surprise at all—than to see him act as if he could, like a mute who repeatedly opens his mouth in the hope that words will come out.

I snuck out the back way, kicked the dog out of its nest of filthy old blankets, and the two of us started up to the corner dairy on High Street. I was bound to run into someone I knew, hopefully someone with stolen money. I was thinking I would like something to eat, not food as such, but maybe some chocolate, or milk bottle lollies, or a coconut-ice bar or some spearmint leaves. I might even look over the iceblocks.

Then the dog saw a cat, and a woman I didn't know screamed at me from a house that was usually shut up, and I forgot Dad and the piano.

Amid the shouting and the woman's screaming I grabbed hold of the dog's bullish neck with both hands. This was the same little puppy I'd let piss over my bare stomach. Now it wanted to tear that cat apart. The woman bent down and the cat leapt into her arms. She stroked the head of her shitty cat. She called out some abuse and backed into her house and shut the door.

In the ringing silence the air smelt of cat fear and in my head were the shiny surfaces of the piano and my father's grey eyes straining for notes that he could not find, that he would never find, not then or in a thousand years.

Two big events within five minutes—the world has gone mad.

I need to reinvigorate myself, and so decide to backtrack and wander along the cutting from Taita Drive that the retarded kid used to take to get to our back fence. Half of the fence is now eaten away, and as I pass it I wonder what has happened to him as I never see him any more. He goes into that box of sudden departures never explained. This is two or three years before the pregnant girl at school is abducted by aliens. The dog is in one of its unseemly jaunty moods after the cat episode and pads alongside me. There is the lively smell of fennel and a whiff of the illegal rubbish dump. The track leads past the golf course and down to the river.

I drop onto the tee nearest the houses and wander onto the fairway to a big windbreak of soft firs. It is hard to tell one tree from the next; they have been planted so closely that the ends of their branches interlace. I leave the dog sniffing and scratching behind its ear while I climb to the top of one of the trees. I'm high enough to feel a slight breeze which was barely noticeable on the fairway. I can see all the way to the river. In the other direction are the tiled roofs of the houses. Beneath my feet, the dog gazes up at me through the shredded branches. It knows the drill. At a moment of my choosing, which I cannot predict and which has no pattern, I simply let go, and free-fall—crashing through the under-layers.

I feel as though I have returned to the full dominion of self, and fear like some internal wind fills me out. But I know I will be caught by a lower branch. The fear is fleeting, and the not knowing is illusory.

My father, as a boy, was not so lucky.

The extremely rare event of a car pulling into his street is a sign that his time was up. He must go inside and pack his bag. A stranger is on his way to take him to another house where more strangers will line up in the hall by the front door and stare at him with ragged smiles.

He will be shown to a new bed in a new room. There will be new procedures to learn, a new family to work his way inside, to understand, and then one day he will hear a car pull into the drive and look up to see a stranger get out and stretch and find him with a look that my father instantly knows is for him, not the dog, or the woman standing sheepishly by the door. Inside he goes to pack his bag. On the porch a hand drops onto his shoulder, in another awkward farewell.

When I am ten years old, for reasons baffling to me, my father gets in the car and drives off to the Epuni Boys' Home and returns with a boy a year older than me carrying a battered suitcase.

The idea, as it is put to me, is to give me company since my brother and sisters have moved out long ago. But I never asked for company, and besides I have all the friends I need; plus there's the dog, the silly bugger, bewitched by his tail, driven wild by it, turning in circles until he finally gets a hold of it in his jaws and won't let go and crabs across the lawn with his arse in his mouth. What could be more diverting than that? And then there's Rex the salamander, and the launching of myself out of treetops.

I imagine the kid came to live with us because of another conversation that I was never privy to, as well as a shared desire to give an unloved orphan a better childhood than perhaps either Mum or Dad had enjoyed.

My sister Lorraine and her baby, Nicole, are still living in the caravan in the Hutt Park campground, so the new kid is given her old bedroom. It's just across the hall from the toilet, but the boy from the home still manages to wet the bed every other night. No matter how many times he washes and bathes he still stinks of piss. He also steals from my friend's mother's handbag (but then so does her son, who many years later will wind up in Long Bay jail in Sydney for car conversion). Still, it's embarrassing. And at a screening of *The Sound of Music* the embarrassment reaches new excruciating heights when, in his strange husky voice brimming with indignation at the failure of von Trapp to finish the Lord's Prayer in the usual way, the kid from the home bellows out for the whole picture theatre to hear, 'He forgot to say "Amen!"'

How did he know that? On the way home I try not to look at him. The way he sits is irritating. He is pissing me off even more than he usually does. He is perched on the edge of the back seat, leaning forward; his freckly face, which I don't like, is raised and tilted back to an unnecessary degree, and his bottom jaw is unhinged and his mouth hangs open.

In his room there are two beds. The one that he has taken is pushed against the wall behind the door, so that on opening the door the room appears empty, a joy to find, but then I get a whiff of that old piss smell and when I look around the corner there he is, there he still was, looking sorrowful, like a dog that knows that you know it has farted.

I couldn't wait for him to leave. Nine months after unpacking his pyjamas in Lorraine's old bedroom he is returned to Epuni Boys' Home.

For a number of days I kept his bedroom door closed. Eventually I opened it, and the window, and it was like he was never there.

Stephen was his name.

I like to think that had everything been explained differently, had I known something of my father's childhood, I would have shown more patience, more tolerance. But I never guessed the reasons behind what seemed an inexplicable thing to do— bring a strange kid in to the house and then pretend that it was all perfectly normal.

~

It was raining again and the carriage windows fogged up, and Wales disappeared from view. I was left with the solitary smell of the train. I closed my eyes and thought back to the shiny new piece of furniture in the house and, following the tentative notes down the hall, my shock to find Dad sitting in a trance at the piano, his thick welder's fingers resting on the keys.

Wales didn't speak to me. Or perhaps it did and I couldn't hear it properly, unfamiliar with its fluted notes, unable to tell the subdued from that which barely seemed to exist. Wales. It smiled weakly in the way of relatives who have fallen out of touch and know they are supposed to recognise each other but aren't certain any longer of who it is they are speaking to.

The philosopher Ludwig Wittgenstein once collated the photographs of his siblings and cousins and with the help of a photographer friend overlaid them to produce 'a family look'. In Wales I did see a kind of sloped shoulder and catch a round-at-the-shoulder look, an evasiveness that wished to see everything but did not wish to be observed in turn. I saw myself, in other words.

There was something else, too, that seemed to reflect me inside out. The moment, however, I try and single it out or fillet it into parts that can be described or named such as nose, cheekbone, or eyes, the observation falls apart. I can't be more precise. Except to point out the uncanny feeling of familiarity I felt in a place that I had never visited. That is what it was like in Wales. A slow leaching between myself and that which I observed, until I too could have been shuffled into a pack of locals, *a la* Wittgenstein, without polluting the 'representative look'.

Such a possibility does not excite me; it means some less than desirable things claiming membership within my personal constituency and cultural memory—a shabbiness and a decent proportion of sour shadow, the gruffness of station masters, the crappy food and malfunctioning toilets (often mysteriously locked), the unionised operation of the food cart, the filthy-arsed sheep I saw through the train window that spoke of a certain sloppiness. The song and dance and pissy-eyedness of the place also goes into the mix.

And were I to suffer a personal earthquake and be split open, I am quite certain a team of awkward blokes would scramble out of me with a pint in one hand and a balled fist in the other, and that the temptation to fight would be confused with one to sing. Another mob would split to the hills without so much as a backward glance, and a smaller constituency would make for the ridges and beneath a low sky set a course for the distant headland.

I might throw in a dash of stoicism that began with a line of sea mariners and farm labourers arriving on the far side of the world to emerge in the form of my father. The stoicism seems to have stopped with him. It wasn't passed on to his children, and in any case we would have shrugged it off like some foul and soiled garment. No, we don't waste a moment if we feel our own situation can be made better by screaming and shouting about it.

Dad, on the other hand, set off in the dark each day in the foulest weather, not especially bothered because, after all, it is July, and in July it rains. He would step off the porch and his hat brim would start to spill with the cold rain without his seeming to notice it. The one time in his life that he was unshackled from the factory and his soldering irons was when he was a gold prospector in the 1930s. It was the only part of his past I heard him talk about. For food he shot deer, and when moved by an appetite for a trout he threw a stick of gelignite into the river.

Once, when I was ten years old, he took me down to the goldfields. We stopped in a pub in the middle of nowhere. Dad talked with the barman. I must have looked away or been diverted by the pig's head on the wall and when I looked back I saw a glass jar of nuggets sitting on the bar. We drove to the goldfields, parked at the end of a road and set off over paddocks.

I saw a lamb born. It was breech and Dad had to reach in with his hand and turn a few knobs before he got the lamb out. It was covered in a yucky yellow skin. We watched it get to its feet. It shook a bit. Then it opened its eyes. I have an idea it saw Dad, with a stub of a cigarette stuck to his lip, before it saw its mother. It must have wondered what sort of world it had arrived at and how the family look could vary so wildly.

We carried on across the fields, scrambled down a bush track and on the river flats came to a large sluicing pipe. Now that Dad had the scent of the place in his nostrils, he scrambled here and there. I followed after to find him looking in a concentrated way at something that on its own was nothing more than a bank or a rock pool and once, I recall, a tree. We climbed up another track and came out of the bush to a paddock scattered with stones. They turned out to be the foundations of dwellings that had burnt down or blown away in the wind. I followed him around from one lot of stones to the next until he stopped, satisfied that this was the place where he had slept for three years on the ground. In the dry grass I counted four stones set in a square. Each man had a side to himself. I asked him which side was his, and he nodded at a particular line in the grass. I didn't think to doubt him. But now that he had found the spot there wasn't much more to do than look at the ground and take in the world from that position. It was like being on a train going through Wales. Time slowed on the back of a long obligatory examination.

Some years later I was to roam a hillside that creeps down

from Bendigo Station to Lake Dunstan in Central Otago in the South Island where a community of Welsh gold prospectors and their families had stuck it out for twelve years. The remnants of their stone cottages and a big sluicing operation still stand, along with a church and a school and a number of stony tracks that connect one cottage with another up and down the hillside and over a stream of good drinking water.

There was a clear sky, no wind, and although spring had only just begun it was surprisingly hot. But in winter the water pools iced over. Those Welsh miners and their families must have called upon a certain fortitude to get them through.

My father's default expression was one of vacancy. Hot tar could have been poured inside his skull and he would not have complained. His hands were covered with thick skin from handling steel. I saw him pick up gorse in his bare hands. I suppose if you empty yourself out there is nothing left to scald or hurt. I don't have his forbearance, but I do have the expression that goes with it.

On the journey through Wales I saw that expression on faces lining station platforms—a vacant look, bordering on gloom.

~

It was raining in Swansea too. When we stopped at the station I could barely see out the windows. Then we were leaving, thank God, and as the train came off a bridge—I think it was a bridge; there was a lovely sense of elevation and of launching away from the city—we punched out of the grey rain and came into sunshine, and, just ten minutes on from Swansea's bleak doorway, there appeared a vast estuary of wet sand and fast-moving currents. A gap opened in the coastal hills and my eyes shot to the horizon and back again to the sand flats that were rapidly moving from one state to the next with the historically minded way of tides.

Then, as though the carriage window had been struck by seagull shit, a caravan park popped up, at odds with everything seen so far, and the train headed inland, to rolling green hillsides and long hedgerows that trickled down the slopes.

A shadow like a dark pond on a distant hill moved on with the cloud.

Shadows everywhere, striding out of the valleys.

Three-quarters of me is from here. I have to keep remind-ing myself of that fact. Three-quarters of me turns out to be a stranger. I am the tail end of a vanished comet.

I wonder what has passed on to me—what I have unwit-tingly absorbed. Sideburns, wispy hair tailing off behind the ears, a susceptibility to colds and bold offerings, a taste for sweet things, a policeman's plodding look, but also an attraction to the anarchic, not so much a torching of trees but setting fire to the rubbish tip behind the house, after which we hid in a tight cluster of broom and snuggled up to its cartridges of black seeds terrified at what we'd done as the fire engines screamed their way to the blaze. A general rage—at varying targets: genocide, shabby cafe service, someone's elbow drifting into my space on an aeroplane—an irritability more or less constant, like a wavering magnetic needle. I have no idea what my father's father, the man who drowned at sea, looked like.

My mother had what used to be called a 'Roman nose'. I suppose she must have got it from her mother or father. It's hard to tell from the photographs of Maud. She looks like she's trying to put out the torches of a witch-hunt with a disarming smile. So the nose, to the extent it shows, is diminished. Perhaps Mum inherited it from the farmer. And what of him has passed down to me? A photograph would be useful. A photograph might tell all. Then I could peer into it until my own features might begin to arrange themselves in his, and a bit of reverse colonisation would be achieved—if I had such a photograph.

Photographs of course are not always reliable. Just as a landscape can change, so can a face. When my mother was forty, just before she had me (and came down with toxaemia *as a result,* she said), a dentist, with some authority, suggested she would be better off without her teeth, so he pulled them all out. It had been presented to her as a future saving. There would be no dentist bills. Also, false teeth were a very modern solution. I quickly became accustomed to the sight of her teeth, left to stand in a glass of water, usually a recycled Marmite jar, on a table beside her bed. When I went into her room to do my spelling before school, the teeth would be in that jar of water. Mum was learning Esperanto at the time. I suspect she probably had some success with that useless language with her teeth out—a language with no home, a bit like those teeth sitting cartoonishly in a glass.

There was a moment on the train when I looked out and imagined an intersecting view of myself and 'the man who drowned at sea'. Our sightlines fell on the same white cottages, the same boggy weald, the sky, in flight for one and welcoming the other. Fanciful, of course, because in spite of the self-reflective substance bouncing in the window for most of the time I felt apart, as you do on a train, when the upwinds you float on are deeply individualised and the country looked out upon is confused with other landscapes.

A woman I know in the shoe factory buys a lotto ticket every week. I like to tease her about it. Play the worldly sceptic to her resilient faith in miracles. On my way through Wales I wondered what she would make of me now, on my way to a place that used to be a place in the hope of that incendiary moment of sudden illumination when origins would flare up into the present. She would be too kind to laugh as I do at her lotto-buying habit.

At least half a dozen times I felt like getting off the train— the first was outside Newport when the windows misted over. It was a shock to discover how easily the will to carry on drained from me. Then came a moment at a railway crossing—I forget where. The clouds parted and, as the bells rang, the surrounding fields came to life. I felt a powerful urge to get off. I was tired of the train. I wanted to step into the picture, find a pub and sit down at an outside table with the newspaper and a beer. I pushed my face closer to the window, and a train came from the other direction. It shook the carriage, then passed, and everything went still in that post-trauma way. The bells stopped, and the train got on its way again to Pembroke Dock.

I was a bit tired of myself, as much as of the train. I was tired of Rooney, the Man U striker scowling up at me. I picked up the newspaper. I wanted to find a bin. But then I thought I might as well take a look first, which is how I came upon a story about a farm labourer preying on hikers along the Pembroke Coast.

The man's murderous brutality brought to mind Joseph Dally, who, more than twenty years ago, kidnapped a teenage girl off a street quite near the one where I had grown up and drove her around the coast road, where as a child I had walked with Mum and Dad, counting off the bays, desperate for a biscuit. In the bay with the jagged remains of an old wharf, from where the cattle would be shipped across the harbour in the killing season, we often stopped for a biscuit, and that's where Dally buried alive his young victim. Now, I cannot walk by that shingled beach without a thought for that girl. No number of spread picnic blankets will erase the memory of the spot on that beach. And as the train blasted out of a short tunnel another memory of that very same beach came to me.

I have stolen a bottle of wine from home for a 'picnic' with a girl who is lying on the shingle beside me. Every now and then a wave pushes up to us and drains noisily through the pebbles. The sky moves by. The inter-island ferry veers close enough for us to see the passengers lining the deck. They are looking in our direction but cannot see us. I wonder who, if anyone, saw and waved to Dally as he drove around this coast road. I never thought of the cattle stunned with their throats slit when I saw the harbour red with blood from the meatworks at Ngauranga and Petone. I never thought to make the connection.

~

Years ago when I met Mavis, my mother's first cousin—in other words, the niece of that old ratbag, Maud—she told me that the day she met my mother off the train in Taunton she was so nervous she would rather have had a tooth extracted.

By her own account, and Mum's, the visit was a great success. More so, I suspect for Mum. Mavis had treated her as family. And so a lost button was sewn back into the fabric.

Mavis was standing on her doorstep on Hamilton Road ready to greet me when my taxi drew up outside her house. Slim, grey. In manner very much like my mother.

Inside, Mavis poured me a dry sherry, a drink favoured by Mum until her triumphant discovery of gin-and-tonic. Mavis had the album ready, and before lunch we worked our way through Maud's side of the family—a long line of women bringing up children by themselves, husbands killed in and around wars, a mix of schoolteachers and slightly eccentric stay-at-home types who, I was pleased to hear, couldn't be bothered with work in the conventional sense. They are the ones in the photographs staring into empty paddocks.

It was uncanny how much Mavis sounded like Mum. How does a woman who has barely ever left Somerset end up sounding like a woman born on the other side of the world?

Mavis had won a scholarship to a posh girls' school, and there the locality of accent had been scraped away until she sounded strangely like my mother, who had left school at twelve, but with some conscious effort, I suspect, created a voice for herself that she must have got from the radio.

After a lunch of shrimp we returned to the front room to go through the remaining albums.

Before Maud gave up my mother she had two boys, Ken and Eric, in quick succession to Harry Nash. This might have been the occasion to ask Mavis what she knew of Nash. Was he a gardener or involved with leather? But I didn't think to ask. The photo I lingered over was the one of Maud with her sons. Mavis said Maud visited with the boys after the war, in the early 1920s, and stayed in this same house. I didn't ask the obvious questions. Why? Or whether Maud had mentioned the existence of my mother to her family in England.

I kept looking at that photograph of Maud and her sons. Officially they look complete. Unofficially someone is missing.

~

In the weeks following the February 2011 earthquake, a man on national radio spoke of sifting through the rubble of the family home and finding his grandfather's accounting certificate from

1937. I would bet that if he had ever been asked to compile a list of his most precious things an accounting certificate would not have been on it, yet the joy in his voice was clear.

I was back to feeling hopeful of what I might find in Pembroke Dock. I wanted it to be affirming in some way—a surprise, like the accounting certificate found in the rubble.

I warned myself about being overly critical. An interior voice completely unfamiliar in its wisdom advised me just to let things come to me.

As the train slowed at Tenby some middle-aged hikers in woollen hats and scarves battled their way to the front of the carriage. I watched them regroup on the platform, mounted with day packs, clutching walking sticks. While they stamped their feet to shake off the torpor of the train, I stared with an impolite interest, as I used to at Rex the salamander, noting the colour of their faces, their bone structure and the unflattering sack-like quality of their bodies, like things to be filled and dragged here and there. The more I looked the more I saw the scrapyard of genetic origin. There was a woodland quality to those faces out on the platform. They listened more than they spoke and looked greedily self-aware.

Then as we left Tenby I saw something which, like some moment of deep embarrassment, I cannot shake.

I happened to glance down at the painted lines of an empty car park. They were quite wrong. By that I mean there was something odd about them. Carpark convention had been discarded but not, as far as I could see, for any useful gain.

Instead of broken lines painted at the usual intervals these had been turned into rectangles by an over-conscientious fellow with a paint brush. It was the kind of needless attention to the wrong detail which, unkindly at that moment, I associated with a father who had once built me a cart so heavily engineered that when it attained speed there was no stopping it, and many a time I had to eject myself from behind the wheel and throw myself onto a neighbour's dog-shit-covered lawn just before the steel contraption cannoned into the tin fence at the end of the street.

I wished I hadn't seen those stupid rectangles at Tenby, because when I thought who on earth could fuck up a simple task such as painting lines onto the tarseal of a car park I realised, shatteringly, that I could.

Then we came into Pembroke—small, countrified, stone buildings, nodding fields, a hint of the sea.

There were just two of us left in the carriage. The other remaining passenger was a great big jellyroll of a man who for several hours had sat slumped at the far end of the carriage. When he stood to make his way along the aisle I feared for him, as he looked quite capable of bursting catastrophically out of himself but for the clothes and belt at full strain. I found myself staring at the piles of collapsed flesh, caught and held in various places over his torso, and out on the platform, where my eye followed him, I saw the welcoming folds in the hills.

As the train left Pembroke the view across the aisle opened up to flat land, and there between two lumps of hill was a line of sea, blue as I hoped it would be.

Pembroke Dock has a sort of Gilbert and Sullivan ring about it, which is appropriate given what spilled out of there.

For a long time we believed my father's father, Arthur Leonard Jones, was born in a dockyard of cranes and broken warehouses between the cries of seagulls and curses and ship whistles, a birthplace combining the urgency of imminent departure with the steadying and becalming effect of the wharves.

We would also say with absolute conviction that it was normal for British naval officers to record the dock as the birthplace of their offspring. Somehow it was known—or else it had been decided—that Arthur's father was a British naval officer. And so his birthplace has always suggested itself as a place too lacking in community roots to qualify as a proper place. It never occurred to me that Pembroke Dock is more than a dock, extending beyond the high walls of its historic waterfront to include a town and steep hillsides that look out to the Irish Sea.

After briskly leaving the railway station I came to a halt by some shops, and thought, 'Now what?' On the train my destination had never been in doubt, but now I was here it seemed less than precise. There was no address to look up or door to knock on. And now that I was here I didn't know what to do, except to look like someone who knew what to do and how to proceed, and so in this imitative state I picked up my bag and walked on. I looked around but nothing I saw stuck for more than a few seconds. It felt like one of those hopeless errands where you have been sent to fetch someone you have never met from a crowded train station. I stopped again, and held my nose to the air, and then, I recall, I did recognise something. It was the sea air. It came sweeping along the main street. I picked up my bag and headed in the direction it came from.

Soon I found myself looking up at the impressive and robust stone walls of the dockyard. A bronze relief depicted a predatory crowd of merchants and wives waiting outside the gates on pay day. This is how it was at 20 Stellin Street. Dad brought home the pay packet and handed it over to Mum, who gave him a bit of pocket money for tobacco. On the bronze, the workers in their cloth caps drag their downward faces out to meet the crowd. I'd seen men with those faces before, crammed in to the back of our car. Dad sat in the front, Mum behind the wheel. The shoulders of three other welders jammed up against me in the back. And no one spoke—not a word—until the car slowed down and stopped, the back door creaked open, and there was a tired *thanks Joyce, see you Lew.* Then the silence again, a silence pounded out of drudgery, was poured back into the closed air of the car, and off we went to the next house, the car getting lighter at each stop, like a change of seasons, until it was just us, and an opportunity for Mum to ask Dad, 'So how did it go today?' Although I don't remember her ever asking that question.

I followed the walls down a steep road to the harbour, and there I stood on a stone embankment where I took everything in: the air now came from a place further out to sea, but retained some tinctured familiarity that I traced to the tresses of heavy brown kelp shifting beneath my feet against the stone sides of Pembroke Dock. It was mid-tide, and across the bay I could see the high-water marks on the beach and, higher up, a perfectly white lighthouse stood against a shadowed hill, the top third of it dominating the skyline—and yes, it might as well have been the lighthouse back at Pencarrow. The sun came out and Pembroke Dock lit up. The hills turned a dazzling green, and the blues of the harbour leapt. I could see a way to scramble up the hillside to the lighthouse, but there wasn't time. I had decided there wasn't any. The train was leaving in forty-five minutes and just now, or perhaps a few minutes earlier, or maybe when I stood before the dockland walls taking in the bronze relief of the workers, I had decided that I wanted to be on it.

Did the ghost of Arthur Leonard Jones look on with a mirthful smile? But from where? A shop doorway? The docks? The bronze relief? I could not find him in that cloth-capped crowd. From a sloping deck? But there were no ships or sailing vessels in the harbour, other than the large creamy sides of the Irish ferry, and I didn't look there. I couldn't find whatever space he had fallen out of. Nowhere screamed out, 'Here I am!'

I can't really explain the sense of urgency to be on that train. Except to say it was the equal of the determination that saw me travel all this way to this southwest port in Wales.

As kids we used to dive to the bottom of the sea and bring up a fistful of sand as proof that we had touched the bottom.

In Pembroke Dock I had touched the bottom. Now I found myself looking wildly around for something to take away. Something good and solid, I hoped, a touchstone for whenever Pembroke Dock was mentioned in the future.

It came to me while I stood at the harbour's edge. The cloud drifted away, and the sun found the sea. I looked across to the hills and saw the lighthouse at Pencarrow and the landscape merge and shift apart again. The shadow of one became instantly filled with the presence of the other.

And then I started to run like hell back to the station.

~

The seats in the carriage were still facing Pembroke Dock. It was as if I had been expected. Then as we moved out I felt a bit regretful. Perhaps like Arthur Leonard Jones I was being impulsive. The sun broke through again and I noticed the wild flowers in the paddocks and the whiteness of the walls; then it slid behind a thick cloud and everything turned back to murk, and the regret lifted. Hard-won impressions and other minor bits of evidence drifted out of my head until Pembroke Dock was once again a place that used to be a place on the birth certificate of a grandfather I never met.

Solitary houses appeared, like breakaway republics. The grander houses strained to break out of the averageness of their own conceit. They were narrow in beam where there was absolutely no need to be. Acres of farmland surrounded each one. It was as though they didn't wish to impose or to take more space than a terrace house, which is actually what they looked like—terrace houses lifted out of the tight huddle of neighbourliness and dropped onto empty paddocks. Here and there, a white farmhouse rose above a distant hedgerow to offer a rural point of view. Closer to the tracks in narrow creeks, stood lethargic cattle. The reflection of the train flashed by in dark ponds. A pre-industrial sky appeared, a patch of Georgian blue, fluffy white clouds. I half expected a woman in a bonnet clutching a basket of eggs to wave up at the rushing windows.

I wonder about the life-changing decision of the emigrant to leave behind tight clusters of habitation. I imagine heated discussion about the merits of the new life heard through five sets of walls, the rumour mill beginning shortly after, then the grim farewells conducted in the mood of a funeral. And, as in death, the names of the departed talked about, remembered at odd times, then not at all, their absence registered in that way that a roaring wind marks the place where forests once stood.

~

Some years ago my sister Pat began to delve into our family history. It was a time when documents held by government ministries were accessed only with great difficulty and persever-ance. One Christmas she produced for Mum and the rest of us a blue cloth book containing birth and death certificates, some letters, a few newspaper articles. For the first time we knew the name of Mum's father. Pat's efforts also flushed out the Bibbys, the parents of Eleanor Gwendoline Jones, Dad's grandparents and my own great grandparents, as they are but as I never knew them to be.

At the time the blue book came into existence my notion of family was confined to my immediate one. The Bibbys sat too far back in the story and lacked the mythic charge that might have made me sit up and take notice.

I was more impressed by my wife's family history. Its evidence was everywhere—in photographs, on home movies, in story—some of it worked up to myth. Such as Max, jailed for revolutionary activity in Russia in the 1880s, his escape made possible by his mother singing instructions up to his cell window in Yiddish. Max's brother Joe had a scar on his face made by a cutlass. On account of the scar, my wife's father, Jerry, always thought Joe was the hero. In fact, Scarface had dobbed in his brother. I was also impressed by the fact that my wife's grandmother had been one of the first female pharmacists in Brooklyn, New York, and that she used to sell heroin to the Mob over the counter and was licensed to carry a firearm, which she did, as shown in the photographs, holstered to the outside of her dress.

Our family story comprised little more than a list of names, and none with a flair for anything.

But, on my second time through Swansea, I suddenly remembered the Bibbys.

John Bibby, 'mariner', and his sixteen-year-old wife, Mary,

both illiterate, appear on the register of assisted immigrants aboard the *Asia*. They sailed from Tilbury Dock in 1874 to try their luck in the raw Otago settlement of Kaitangata.

In a newspaper report of an assault case against Great-Grandfather Bibby, he is referred to as a 'farmer', a generous description for the owner of a 'modest section' bought as part of the Cemetery Reserve block sale. In another report he appears as 'a settler'. And, a 'flax-cutter' in a longer report of a case where his name appears as a suspect in an arson attack on a neighbour's stack of 'oaten shaves' valued at £100.

Bibby had taken exception to a suggestion by an inspector from the Rabbit Control Board that he wasn't doing his bit to keep the local rabbit population down, and, consequently, felt a strong urge to punch the man. In the arson hearing, a rabbiter working in the area where the fire occurred said Bibby was a regular sight on the hill and, ten days before the fire, had told him that his neighbour, a man named Smith, 'could cut his throat if he got the chance, but he [Bibby] would do some harm to him some day'. Bibby denied the claim that he and Smith were on bad terms. He said he'd never made threats to his neighbour or any other person. He then said he did not remember saying to the rabbiter that Smith could cut his throat and that he would injure him. But he 'would not sware [*sic*] that he had not said so'.

'The defendant made a long rambling statement,' the article continues, 'endeavouring to prove provocation.'

The *Clutha Leader* concludes with the jury's decision: 'The stacks (with a value of one hundred pounds) had been wilfully set on fire by some person to them unknown.'

Bibby may well have had a motive. In another article he is the victim of arson. In the night he is woken by dogs barking and discovers his stack containing eighteen to twenty bushels of oats on fire. While attempting to put out the fire he hears the movement of a man in nearby scrub. The man runs off; Bibby gives chase but loses him. The article also provides some detail about the marriage. The Bibbys sleep in different bedrooms. Mary Bibby had moved out once before 'in consequence of some words with him', but also after their pigs were poisoned and some property was stolen. Several times Bibby had asked her to return; finally he prevailed, only for this arson to rekindle her distress. The newspaper article also mentions that before their move to their current address the Bibbys had lived briefly in Milton, where their house, insured, had burnt down.

Why should I care if he was guilty or innocent? Curiously, I did care. A niggling doubt about Bibby's role—his evasiveness and rambling statement—perhaps has something to do with my own trickle-up or trickle-down misdemeanours, such as setting fire to the rubbish dump at the back of the house at 20 Stellin Street. I wonder if waywardness can be inherited. I wonder if Bibby was a bit of a hot head. I feel it might be true.

It had been thrilling to see the rubbish dump go up in flames. Just as it had been thrilling when I threw all the firewood patiently collected and stacked by a man and his grown-up son into the Hutt River. I'd hidden in the bushes so I could watch their reaction. That was really the point of the exercise, but it became less exciting when father and son looked around and quickly split to circle behind my position and flush out 'the little prick'. The prick was marched to the riverbank. Father and son debated what to do next. The son wanted to throw 'the prick' into the river. The father spoke of driving 'the little prick' to the police station. In the end, after soliciting my telephone number so they could ring the prick's parents (naturally I gave them a wrong number) they let the prick go.

~

The newspaper articles and a coroner's report also provide detail of Bibby's mixed fortunes. From milling timber and building props for the nearby Castle Hill coalmine he has saved enough to begin building 'a good-sized cottage' when he is struck down.

In no particular order he cuts his finger on a chafing knife, is knocked off his horse by an over-hanging branch, is thrown from his horse and lands on a tree stump and then, with his foot caught in the stirrup, is dragged along the ground. The incidents read like a series of indignities. One of his injuries, however, will lead to an excruciating death in 1894 by tetanus.

The coroner was unsure, at first. Bibby's symptoms suggested either strychnine poisoning or tetanus. To add to the confusion, the correspondent for the *Clutha Leader* reports 'an epileptic fit' as the cause of death. If correct, here is the source of Lorraine's epilepsy, as it is carried through the male line.

Mother and daughter describe a strange mood overtaking Bibby. He seems abstracted, unreachable. His wife recalls him often depressed and prone to sitting around the house lamenting the decision to buy in Kaitangata instead of staying in Milton. He complains of rheumatism, until it reaches the stage where he can barely move his arms and legs. His nine-year-old son describes him on a milling expedition lying down in the bush unable to move. At night he wakes screaming, his body in convulsion. The fits increase until at last he agrees to see a doctor.

Dr Fitzgerald found him calling out in pain and grasping a rope with his right hand. Bibby wouldn't let the doctor touch him:

> He said each touch brought on one of those turns he had had. I found him bathed in perspiration, his shirt being simply soaked. His pulse was rather rapid, pulsations being about 108 per minute. He complained greatly of thirst. His wife gave two sips of water. While still on his bed he took a fit of vomiting and vomited about two or three ounces of clear fluid. Almost directly after one of the vomits he took a fit, and while the fit was on his face was livid. He did not froth at the mouth nor bite his tongue and seemed conscious all through it. He took a second fit much more severe from which he did not rally.

Dad's mother, Eleanor, is sent to the local hotel to identify her father's body—presumably there was no hospital—and there, in the hotel, two doctors saw through Bibby's skull and cut out the brain to search for clues to his death.

Dr Fitzgerald continues, 'Apart from a slight adhesion to the membrane everything was normal. The upper part of the spinal cord all healthy. The lungs and heart healthy. The stomach was found empty, no trace of poison could be detected.'

The hotel where Bibby's brain was cut out can be found in a watercolour by Christopher Aubrey, painted in 1878, a few years after the Bibby's arrival in Kaitangata. The hotel and church huddle by the confluence of the Clutha and Kaitangata Rivers. To the rear the hills, which presumably Bibby had a hand in clearing, look stiff and paralysed.

~

From Tilbury Dock to Port Chalmers the Bibbys were seventy-eight days at sea. Their immediate world is dense, stifling. A child's cough or runny nose is a worrisome thing. Fear of sickness and especially fever accompanies the endlessness of the journey. After a few weeks of being washed in sea water, clothes have a stiff salted feel, and the flesh crawls with imaginary lice. Sleeping conditions are appalling. People are stacked into impossibly small places, which they enter feet first. These long voyages were perhaps the first step in losing contact with old ways. A child might be sewn into a linen bag and dropped overboard less than two hours after its death, and despatched with the body is that lingering sentimentality more common on land.

I wonder about the tremendous distances that existed in those days and the erasing nature of the ocean—that vast and bland divide between past and future—and the effect on the Bibbys of a journey where the land went missing for weeks on end, before, suddenly, there it is, like a monstrous surprise, and where so much is seen for the first time, so much that is unfamiliar, perhaps spectacular. But how much of it is retained in the minds of the illiterate? How might meaning be attributed or memory preserved in the absence of diaries, journals, cameras, canvases, sketchpads? Things don't get written down. Observation and eloquence come from official sources—the captain, the surgeon, the church minister.

I wonder if the assault on the Rabbit Board inspector resulted from bluster on Bibby's part. The inspector has reached into his pocket for a document, and to cover up the fact that he cannot read Bibby finds a way to shift things into an area where he knows how to conduct himself.

Another generation on and that scoundrel Arthur Leonard Jones will make the same ocean journey. He will meet and marry John Bibby's daughter, my grandmother.

If I'd paid closer attention when the blue book first came into my hands I might have discovered Arthur Leonard Jones's reason for leaving Wales. On his marriage certificate (to Eleanor Gwendoline Bibby) he is described as a 'widower'. He may have wished to put as great a distance as possible between himself and the place of grief. What better place to choose than faraway New Zealand? His wife died in 1897. He married Eleanor in 1903.

A birth certificate, a marriage certificate, a death certificate and an outstanding bill to cover the expenses of the orphanage his kids end up in appear to be the only times he came to official notice. Both he and his parents-in-law, the Bibbys, although for different reasons, are a part of the legacy of silence dumped at the door of 20 Stellin Street, together with an enormous capacity to forget.

In Kaitangata the Bibbys hold two lives within themselves. A third, if childhood is included as country already passed through. On the far side of the world there are new transactions. Layers of observation and memory shift back and forth, between the old and the new, between the place left and the place arrived at, until a sharper impression rises from the broth—this hill is a bit like that one, this bit of Kaitangata is a bit like that bit of Swansea, and if not, then reshaping things until the ingredients of memory disappear into the place of settlement.

But I also wonder if ancestral silence is a form of stage fright.

At primary school, some poor tremulous kid was always being hauled off the mat and stood in front of the rest of us to present a news item. I remember one boy pissing himself. On another occasion, a girl burst into tears. Pissing yourself or bursting into tears didn't seem at all unreasonable. I lived in fear of the teacher's eye beckoning me up into that exposed place in front of the class.

I was in a similar situation to my forebears arriving at a small unknowable place on the other side of the world. What could those faces peering back see in me that I couldn't see for myself? For one thing I didn't trust the sound of my voice. I was unsure where it came from, even less certain that it was truly representative of me.

Then arrived the moment of crisis. My mind turned blank. What did I have to say? I didn't have anything to say. I'd lost the will to speak. Shame rose, like sap, inside me. In the eyes of my classmates I sensed a cruel excitement.

To make things worse I was trying to rid myself of a speech defect. I struggled with my *th*'s. I suspect it had come about after trying to sound like someone else, possibly one of the voices on television I heard through my bedroom door. I used to blame the Irish comedian Dave Allen. But I realise now that he spoke of 'tings' rather than 'fings'. The point remains, however; at 20 Stellin Street the groove of speech was very lightly indented. The dominant voices were the ones on the television ringing through the house. I imagine that is how I came temporarily to lose the *th* sound. Someone like Steptoe bellowing through my bedroom door with his rag-and-bone voice. It seemed to happen without my being aware of it. I found myself talking about *fings* and *foughts*. And even when I realised what had happened I couldn't shake the habit. I'd mislaid the *th* and now I had to make a conscious effort to join up this crucial frontispiece with my things and thoughts. In amazingly quick time I had shed something and the absence of it now revealed me differently to the world, in a way that I didn't especially care for.

I don't want to say *fing* or *fought* so I have to pause and dig around for the *th* sound and attach it to the word before the sentence can safely leave my mouth. A hesitancy creeps into my speech and with it a kind of delayed cognitive response. Instead of leaping fearlessly from subject to subject I have become timid, afraid I will say *fing*. I have turned into a stammerer, without the actual stammer, and in place of speech there arrives instead a sort of closed breath.

~

In London, I saw a man turn himself inside out as he hunted for words to deliver to an audience that had turned up to hear a free 'talk'. It began promisingly: a young woman representing the gallery welcomed the artist Martin Creed, and a man with no arse at all, in a fire engine top framed by a dark vest, leapt on stage, and the audience—twenty-nine of us, as I recall—clapped politely. I had never seen a man who wasn't already dead with so little colour in his face. His head seemed to be abnormally large. It wasn't helped by that hair of his—more like foam— which, of its own initiative, as it seemed, had acquired dramatic personality of its own. So that both the hair and Martin Creed approached the microphone. Then arrived a moment of crisis that was very familiar. Whatever he had intended to say had gone clean out of his head. His mouth closed, and he walked quickly away from the microphone. The eyes of the audience stalked him to the corner of the stage where he stood with his back to us, presumably to collect himself and make a fresh start.

After a few minutes of exhilarating silence, he returned to the microphone to make a fresh start. When eventually he spoke it was slow, agonising, but beautiful too, the way the words seemed to catch—some Scots can do that, sound like their words are drawing through a pit of gravel. He said, 'Someone once told me, that if you don't know what to do, it's best not to do anything.' We laughed—some of us uproariously, as though a horse had just burst out from a barn door and run through a line of washing. We wanted to encourage him, and for the first time Creed smiled. He began to nod, and his attention settled more broadly.

'Did you pay to come today?'

We shook our heads.

'Aye,' he said. 'That's good.'

Another silence rolled out, and I detected a shift in the mood of the audience, a hardening of consumer entitlement. A man down the front sitting in a row by himself crossed his arms in an aggressive manner. This was answered by Creed dropping a hand onto his hip and raising his eyes to the ceiling and slowly shaking his head. Then, the change that came over him made the audience sit up. He strode across the stage and bent to pick up a guitar which I had not known was there until, worryingly, it was in his hands. He set the capo on a high fret and strumming away he sang, 'I don't want to do it. I don't want to do it. I don't want to do it.' Until Creed's 'talk', it had never occurred to me that the presentation of self was a performance and, therefore, every bit as unreliable as the surfaces of a city or a painting, or, for that matter, family history. One observation of Creed's has stayed with me. It came after he explained how the talk had come about; he said he had quite liked being asked, and then there was the newly published book that had catalogued all his work to date that needed to be publicised. 'Aye, the book.' Its mention seemed to depress Creed because he paused. Then he said, 'It's a bit like looking at your shit in a toilet bowl. It's not very nice but sometimes you just have to do it.'

FOUR

WHO, I WONDER, knocked down the door of the Kilbirnie flat to find six children crawling around the corpse of their mother?

Eleanor Gwendoline Jones suffered, as her father John Bibby had, a toxic death, in her case, by hydatids, a disease picked up from contact with dogs. An affectionate lick from a dog is enough to transfer the tapeworm that more commonly infects sheep. Inside the host's stomach the tapeworm grows cysts, some the size of tennis balls, and bigger. For a time the carrier goes about her business, without suspecting anything is seriously amiss. When the cyst bursts, as can happen in a fall, the victim—in this case, my grandmother Eleanor—dies from toxic shock.

Where is her husband, the father to all these kids? A year earlier, Arthur Leonard Jones and Eleanor had separated. Since then, Arthur, described in the blue book as a wharf labourer, appears to have led an itinerant life, leaving a trail of addresses across the city. He is already well on his way to turning into the phantom who will go down in history as a 'naval captain drowned at sea'.

Laura, Dad's eldest sister, is partly responsible for this account. There is a scrap of a letter written by her brother Percy passing on what Laura allegedly told him: 'Our father drowned at sea aboard the SS *Ionic*, a troop-carrying ship, after it was hit by a torpedo off the coast of California.'

Except, everything about that story is wrong. The *Ionic* was fired on, but escaped unharmed and kept sailing. The incident did not occur off the American coast but in the Mediterranean in 1915 with the New Zealand Expeditionary Force on its way to Gallipoli.

I don't doubt that Percy accurately recorded what Laura told him. But where did she hear this story?

On the strength of that 'history', I will develop a strong bond with the sea. I even convince myself that I have innate navigational abilities, which are repeatedly and more success-fully put to the test on land than at sea, finding headlands and coastlines among spires and hilltops.

A different line of inquiry finds Arthur in a hospital bed suffering from sciatica the day his wife is lowered into an unmarked grave in Karori Cemetery, and, later, he turns up in Auckland where he remarries and otherwise leads an obscure life.

~

The woman in the office at the Karori Cemetery keyed in the name Eleanor Gwendoline Jones and with a minimum of fuss printed out her whereabouts, *plot 107*. She showed me on a map where to find her—'at the row beginning Smith, the unmarked grave between Eliot and Wilton'.

I must have always known that my grandmother was buried in Karori Cemetery, but I never went there or paid it any attention because, as far as I can remember, Dad never did. Perhaps the idea of a mother—that particular mother, at least—was as alien to him as a grandmother is to me. I never once heard her name spoken.

Then, in the office, I had another thought. What had happened to Dad's ashes? I remember, after his funeral, stopping on the way to the car park to gaze back in the direction of the crematorium and finding a thin trail of smoke. Edward Llewellyn Jones. The woman keyed in his name. Her eyes trawled down the screen. She looked up, and said, 'His ashes are in the rose garden.' 'On whose authority?' I asked. She put her glasses back on and looked at the screen. 'Mr Robert Jones,' she said. My brother.

The rose garden is below the road opposite the cemetery's admin office. Down there a young runner was going through her warm-down routine. I stared at the roses.

It had never occurred to me to ask about Dad's ashes. Apparently they had been spread without ceremony, or family in attendance.

That wasn't the case with Mum. The last third of her life

was spent at two addresses—a handsome house with a full view of the harbour and a townhouse just before the bend on the road leading out of the bay. In both bedrooms she liked to lie in bed and gaze across the bay and, at night, listen to the police on shortwave radio. I wouldn't have thought she knew much about shortwave radio. But I like the idea of her and the other old ladies along Marine Parade at a sleepless hour tuning their transistors to the static and police-speak, finding comfort in those voices, in their proximity, in the same way that a yawn from the dog in its kennel at night used to banish thoughts of ghosts hanging about in our backyard looking for a way inside the house.

My daughter and I paddled a Malibu surf kayak out to the bay with Mum's ashes on board. I picked a spot she would have been able to see from both houses. The ashes were surprisingly heavy. I poured a stream of white grain into the sea. We paddled in. A few hours later, after lunch at my sister Pat's house, I drove back around the bay. The tide was out a long way, a spring tide, and never have I seen so many gulls in that bay, fighting and diving over the bounty stranded on the sand bars. It was shocking to see, and extraordinary to think that, just a few days earlier, still fully bodied and alert, Mum had lain in bed gazing across this same stretch of water. Without a thought, I am certain, that a few days later seagulls would be squabbling over her ashes.

A day later the gesture felt horribly miscalculated. The sentimentality that led me to paddle her ashes out to sea, the diligent marking of the spot on the tide. What was I thinking? What was wrong with putting her ashes in a jar or burying them in a garden?

From the cemetery office I got in the car and drove deeper into this community of the dead, turning right as instructed by the pedestal with the angel to enter the older part of the cemetery.

I parked, and for the next hour explored the paths between the promised lands and laments, *reunited with Jesus, at rest, joined her husband on this day, entered sleep, drowned at sea*, and so on.

I found a row beginning with Smith and two unmarked graves, one with a dead tree stump resting on it, but there wasn't an Eliot or Wilton in sight, which was disappointing because I liked the wild abandonment of those unmarked plots.

I could sniff rain on its way. It was the edge of a front that was forecast to batter the country over the coming days. I hurried back to the car and drove on until I found a path on the northern side of the hill more closely aligned with the map that the woman in the office had given me.

I quickly found the row beginning with Smith but, as before, could find neither Eliot or Wilton. I checked with the map and was certain I was on the right path. I found one unmarked grave but still no Eliot or Wilton. I walked up and down the rows of headstones. Many of the graves were overgrown, sprouting ngaio and other shrubs. I had to push away the branches and press my fingers into the letters on headstones grown over with lichen. By now it was spitting, so I started back up the hill.

Near the road two leis hung in the branches of a tree shelter-ing a headstone. A woman knelt on a grave with a bucket of water and a scrubbing brush. There were photographs on the headstone of a Samoan woman and a Scotsman. The kneeling woman was scrubbing their grave as though it were a doorstep. I stopped to show her my map to see if she could make sense of it. She said she had just come from visiting her husband's grave at Makara Cemetery, now it was the turn of her parents. A shorthaired dog lay on the next grave. She said she always brought her dog and made a point of introducing herself and the dog to the deceased.

As I drove away from the cemetery I found myself hatching plans for when I find, as surely I will, my grandmother's grave. I will have a headstone erected and inscribed. It won't make any difference to Eleanor Gwendoline Jones. But it will push back the edges of erasure to honour a history that has never been acknowledged.

~

It is a shock to realise how easily the past is disposed of. The man from Pembroke Dock rises from his hospital bed a different man, a single man without responsibilities. He leaves the hospi-tal to find a new world with different possibilities. In a sense he has risen from the dead—a 'drowned Welsh sea captain'—to stumble up the beach to a new and more interesting place where he can start over without the inconvenience of history. He can get on his way again. He can forget Eleanor and all those kids. How many of them. Six? The wind is getting up—look how it dislodges old paper stuck to the road, peeling it off, scattering it. Nothing sticks forever. Nothing—not love, or hygiene, or appetite, not day or night, or the tide. No, wherever he looks, he finds a provisional world. *I am a father* can turn into *I was a father*. He can pretend that Eleanor and the children were a kind of misadventure. As he leaves the hospital gates to walk along Adelaide Road, how new and vital the world smells. Like everyone else in this city he knows how changeable the weather is. In minutes a fine still day in Wellington can turn into a tempest. If it comes to that he will burrow down into the wind, hold his hat low to his face and pick his way around the edge of the city. At the railway station he will buy a ticket to Auckland, and in the new city his resurrection will take full possession of itself.

On his way north, a moment arrives at Kaiwharawhara where the train enters the hillside and pitches into darkness. It is pleasant to be in the dark, even an attenuated dark. To be nowhere in particular loosens any lingering obligation to those irritating bits of responsibility. Then, as the train leaves the tunnel and an enormous light flashes in the window, he blinks, and when he looks again he finds the world changed. The harbour and its plug of sky have been left behind. There is greater latitude in the landscape. It doesn't know him, and he doesn't pretend to know it. And yet there is this other layer, an openness, a welcoming. He is on his way to somewhere—a place he is yet to visit but whose pull is nonetheless irresistible. His recent past can join the general debris of lived moments. There was Pembroke Dock and Swansea, places erased by the crossing of oceans, and Milton, Otago and Wellington, and marriage, and all those children, and those jobs that started and went nowhere. His own self has hardly assembled into a regular and concrete idea; he calls himself whatever the situation requires— labourer, master mariner, naval officer, clerk—and as he passes through each tunnel on his journey north he bursts from the darkness into a new landscape and future.

Sadness will inconveniently erupt now and then. On the back of a child's cry or a child's name shouted in a playground, the past will belch into the present. Perhaps a couple holding the hands of a child will bring competing thoughts of small faces, and of trust and treachery. Perhaps a waitress's smile will remind him of his daughter Laura, and perhaps in a moment's confusion he will call his new wife Eleanor.

～

Dad once told Pat that when he was a small boy he was visited by a man in a naval officer's uniform. He was living in one of many homes in the lower North Island. When the man was leaving, he pressed half a crown into Dad's hand. It was only later, much later, that Dad wondered whether the man in naval uniform was his father.

More likely that person was contracted by the Wellington Industrial School, which had taken over guardianship from the orphanage, to visit my father and report on his wellbeing. Somewhere in a departmental vault lie letters by the boxful detailing the living conditions of Dad and his siblings, charting their prospects and growth in a similar way to the pencil marks on the doorjamb at 20 Stellin Street. I suspect the man in uniform was such an employee. But in Dad's confusion, in the absence of a father, and finding in this adult a grain of kindness in the form of the half crown, perhaps he began to believe that this stranger was not a stranger after all, and conflated two ideals—a father figure and a naval officer capable of avoiding hidden reefs. The visit turned into further evidence of the tale told of the man drowned at sea.

~

The fate of the *Ionic* was published in the *New Zealand Herald* in July 1917. I suspect Arthur Leonard Jones read the article and added a few details of his own, exaggerating one thing in order to achieve the other, a sinking for a drowning, and then perhaps engaged someone to write to the one child unable to verify the record for herself, Laura, who is blind. She disseminates the tale of the naval officer drowned at sea. And so, in his own letter, Percy passes on the myth: 'I found out that our father was a member of the crew of the *Ionic* which was sunk in American waters…all crew and soldiers she was carrying were lost.'

In fact the *Ionic* lived to a ripe old age, and in 1919 Arthur

Leonard Jones rises from the depths of his deception to marry Ada Perrin in Auckland.

~

The 'drowned at sea' line is an old ruse, an honourable despatch, a plausible explanation for unexplained absences. In Nathaniel Hawthorne's novel *The Scarlet Letter*, Hester Prynne is tempted into an affair only after her husband is presumed drowned at sea.

Drowning was a blameless misfortune. Ships thrown off course in violent storms off unfamiliar coasts. It even contained shades of heroism. Our hero, Arthur Leonard Jones, was on his way to the war, battling high seas. The great poet has left behind an uncompleted work. The city has been struck down by a freakish act of nature. Then, the ship's master is discovered to be a drunk. The poet's salted arteries were already closing down before his vision was transcribed. A city discovers its old seismic history and swampy foundations. And Arthur Leonard Jones turns out to be a liar.

~

Following a visit to the orphanage on 117 Tinakori Road, an *Evening Post* reporter wrote approvingly of the conditions he found. 'The children are domiciled until they are fit for transplanting...' He goes on to say, correctly for some but surely not for Eleanor Gwendoline Jones's children, 'The State is the only kind of parent within their memory.' And that the State, in the form of the Industrial School manager, will exercise control over the children until each one reaches the age of twenty-one.

The twins, Jack and Gladys, still babies, are placed with a woman in Todman Street, Brooklyn, in the hills above the city. Dad, Percy and Arthur are placed in the orphanage. Laura is sent to the Institute for the Blind in Parnell, Auckland.

The death of their mother must have been a terrible shock, their delivery into the hands of strangers and institutions another. A series of foster homes will gradually erode the bonds of family—although Jack and Gladys will live near one another in the Manawatu and enjoy a closer relationship than will their siblings. Arthur, the black sheep, is drafted into another life. There is that spell in prison. The blue book mentions a restraint notice from the police preventing him seeing Gladys. Why? No explanation is given.

As soon as they are 'fit for transplanting', that is, to be boarded out for service, each child is issued with a wardrobe the cost of which will be reduced from future earnings.

A boy's outfit consists of:

> 2 pairs of boots (one best, one working)
> 2 caps or tweed hats
> 2 suits (one best, one working)
> 1 extra pair of saddle-tweed trousers
> 1 jersey
> 4 shirts (two best, two working)
> 3 under flannels

2 pairs of braces

3 pairs of socks

6 handkerchiefs (3 coloured, 3 white)

4 brushes (nail, tooth, hair, clothes)

1 comb

1 mirror (optional)

1 pair of leggings

1 oilskin

1 tweed overcoat

2 suits of pyjamas

1 suitcase

2 ties

1 belt

The girls receive a variation of the above:

Woollen singlets

2 working frocks

A workbox containing needles, thimble, pin cushion, scissors, tape, buttons, hooks, cotton and thread and darning wool.

A few other stipulations include the requirement that no girl under eighteen is to be allowed out after 8 p.m. 'An afternoon a week would give as much liberty as is necessary.'

'Boys at service should bear in mind that they are as much under the control of the manager as when they are living at the school.'

'It is very important that the boys should go to church regularly, avoid companions who will lead them to mischief, keep from using foul or coarse language; never go to hotels for drink, nor idle around hotels, billiard rooms, and other places of the kind.'

Their issue of clothes is remarkably like the wardrobe recommended by the New Zealand Company to its migrating passengers. My father and his siblings have been thrown into circumstances that are not of their making. On their way through foster homes, they must, like emigrants, assess the new environment, figure out how things work, pick up new rules and language, and work out tolerances of each place—what can be said, when best to keep one's mouth shut.

~

Most days I cross Taranaki Street and head down to the Moore Wilson supermarket. What a surprise to find it takes me past Dad's birthplace on Jessie Street, just around the corner from the shoe factory. As soon as I found his birth certificate in the blue book I made my way to the address, to discover it is now a car yard. And the boarding house where his grandmother Mary Bibby died is in Cuba Street just around the corner from the shoe factory. I pass by that address most days as well. I've done so for years without ever appreciating the close rub of that forgotten life against my own. The old wooden boarding house where my great grandmother drew her last breath has been replaced by a noodle restaurant.

Whenever I stop to look in the front window I'm sure I give

the impression of a man exploring the curry options. I suppose I have become a familiar sight to the staff and regulars. The face I know best will look up from the counter and smile. One of these days I will go through the doors and order an egg roll. I haven't yet, because that is not part of the routine. To imagine is more compelling. And while I may give the impression of a prospective diner, I am, in fact, dwelling in an upstairs curtained room, lit by a gaslight, and thinking about a fifty-four-year-old woman in bed with childhood memories of Swansea, masted ships, big seas and walks along coastal hilltops, like the one that leads out to Pencarrow, attended to by her daughters, Lucy and Eleanor.

Dr Mackie, who found her on her back on the floor 'in a dying condition', described 'a stout woman, looking more like sixty than fifty-four, and after hearing the history I am of the opinion that the cause of death was cerebral haemorrhaging or apoplexy'.

The building has gone; Mary Bibby has gone; the witnesses have left the premises. The world that accommodated this little exit scene has moved on. But briefly I find myself holding onto that picture before the ferociously lit interior returns me to a table of faces looking back at me. At this point I must either go inside or move on—without, I hope, the maniacal look of Kerrin, the fellow I see wandering the streets around the shoe factory, his electrified eyes also singularly concentrated on the conversation he mumbles to himself.

~

At this pre-dawn hour, Kerrin will have been through the bags of clothes dumped outside the Salvation Army store across the road. So I know where he is now. He's downstairs, at the bottom of the shoe factory, in the atrium waiting for Gib to open up his cafe.

I used to blame the dark for the clothes he fished out of those bags—Kerrin, with his bristling moustache and thick grey rocker's hair, would show up at Gib's in women's slacks and blouses.

On an electoral form Kerrin can tick the Maori and European boxes. Like so many of us, his heritage is a story of mongrels sniffing one another out in a backwater to create a bastard breed incapable of tracing its origins. Actually, I'm just as tempted to describe Kerrin as a wilted flower. You can see the stem, note the petals but hardly recognise the variety. Although the aggression is very familiar. And despite his outrageous getup—purple slacks and weird shoes—his intelligent brown Maori eyes transcend the more embarrassing aspects of himself.

Kerrin is one of Gib's best customers. Gib says he managed to sock a bit away while he slept rough in the hills above Wellington for five years, and so, now, as the city comes into focus and office workers file down through the street below, Kerrin is waiting for Gib to open up so he can start with the first of the ten coffees he will buy today as his rent on a table and chair in the cafe, where he appears to be working at some monstrous opus; whenever I pass the window he is bent over a pile of paper, which Gib says is some sort of musical notation or translation of Maori into English, or perhaps the other way round. For a while I didn't get close enough to see. And then, a week ago, I did. While Kerrin was using Gib's toilet, I turned over the top sheet on the pile, and then the next one, and then I opened the pile at the middle. Every page was written in the same cursive script—a series of joined-up R's smoking away to the edge of the page, resuming on the next line and marching onwards. R after R after R.

I couldn't bear to look at Kerrin after that. And as recently as yesterday morning, each of us looked the other way as we passed in the atrium. Kerrin was imitating someone with purpose, striding out in a column of office workers as they made their way down the lane to Pigeon Park, Te Aro Park as it is now called to acknowledge its pre-European status as an original pā site. This is represented by a waka constructed out of clay tiles. In the rain the hold of the canoe glistens like bathroom tiles. The artwork looks like it flopped out of a failed attempt to capture and remake the past. It is astonishingly vulgar and only hollowly representative. But at least its bathroom-tiled gunwales offer a place for the drunks and assorted street people to while away the day.

Kerrin's challenge is more existential. Each morning he wakes to the question: Who will I be today? And the answer, to some extent, will depend on the clothing fished out of the boxes left outside the Salvation Army store across the road on Ghuznee Street, a minute's walk from Dad's birthplace in one direction and two minutes from the place of his grandmother's death in the other.

~

The smell of liquefaction is like something partially digested and thrown up. The liquefied matter has lost all connection with its original form to turn into nothing in particular. Some thought it smelt like sulphur, although I never heard it said with much conviction. People were just responding to the need to put a word to something apparently indefinable, and sulphur, it seems, was the one foul-smelling element remembered from the periodic table last studied at high school. Of course, there is a scientific explanation, but for the time being it was more satisfying to lurch about in the dark because not to know struck the right chord for an event that no one who wasn't a geologist had been able to foresee. (One geologist had predicted a tragedy resulting from a future seismic event and was accused of scare-mongering.) For everyone else it was like being cast back to the dark ages when things happened and, without a ready explanation, were attributed to a wrathful God.

Yet, if we care to find out, liquefaction has its own story to tell, not so much myth but a creation story nonetheless. Upheaval, displacement, the formation of the plains and swamps and peatlands, the retreat of the sea several millennia ago, the arrival of the podocarp forest and its steady erasure by pastoralists, and then a new weave in the landscape starting with the introduction of farming, followed by the all-conquering cockspur grass and grazing beasts—well, the latter were more cosmetic and scenic, unlike the brew of ancient times, of basalt and shells, and various crustaceans, and peat and swamp turning into coal, and water locked in place by impermeable layers of peat beneath a rock pan, and a network of waterways, some slow, others meandering, others as still as ponds reflecting nothing but the subterranean dark. The liquefaction that sent putrid matter bursting up across the streets of Christchurch was a postcard from these hidden zones.

Nothing had been lost after all, just hidden.

~

The snow and ice in the winter of 2011 had a fossilising effect on the devastation in Christchurch. The pavements around the cordon froze, and the broken city looked like it would remain that way forever.

In August, I returned and entered the red zone, one bridge down from the Bridge of Remembrance. The city streets were deserted. They'd been that way since February. Still, the effect was eerie. The buildings themselves seemed watchful. It was as if a human-like sentience inhabited them—I thought I detected in them a sort of embarrassed awareness of their condition. Here and there a weakened optimism reached out from buildings such as the blistered-looking Grand Chancellor Hotel, with its blown-out windows, and curtains flapping in the breeze. It was like seeing the chest on a corpse suddenly rise.

Inevitably, I made my way to the square in the old heart of the city, where the stone Anglican cathedral half stood, crippled and leprotic. Pigeons flew in and out of gaping holes. The statue of one of Canterbury's founders lay on its side, like a toppled chess piece. The leaves of flora that once flourished here—titoki, mahoe, ngaio, maratara, all wetland plants—were still woven into the texture of Neil Dawson's public sculpture 'Chalice'. Perversely, or justly, this monument to an eviscerated world had come through the carnage intact.

I stood outside the abandoned Heritage Hotel where I had stayed for a night a few weeks after the massive September 2010 earthquake. I was on the top floor, which had made me nervous. I hoped like hell I wouldn't be caught in a subsequent big quake, but consoled myself with the thought it was unlikely because the big one had already happened. Gazing up at its dead windows now, I remembered a pleasant older man in a grey felt hat who was always on hand to open the door with a welcoming smile. On that same trip, following the September earthquake, I had taken a short cut through Press Lane—now it was piled above head height with masonry and rubble. In geological time I had missed being buried alive by a whisker.

I've noticed that whenever people talk about someone they know killed in the February 2011 earthquake they begin with: *He was just on the phone. She had gone outside for a cigarette. She didn't even need to be there. He was helping to move the organ out of the church damaged in the September earthquake.*

I moved up the street from the cathedral and stopped at a window offering breakfast for ten dollars, including hard-boiled eggs. It was the city as normal, you felt, promoted by blue skies and the faint stirrings of spring.

Transform the way you feel. I'd seen that sign in the cracked window of an abandoned hair salon in the suburb of Avondale. In every direction, something indicating faith in the here and now could be found. Old layers of scrim were revealed behind layers of Victorian wallpaper deaf to the racket of jack hammers, while condemned buildings stood in grim lines across from one another. The relentlessness of it was brutal. The giant arms of demolition picked and pecked like cruel insects.

I stopped by a small stone church on a street corner. An engineer holding a clipboard told me it had been steadily crumbling away since the September earthquake. In its destruction it was possible to see how its once elegant form had been composed around the simple act of placing one stone on top of another, like child's play. It had been built with complete faith in its future. Now, just a stump remained.

The next day I wandered through the streets in the eastern suburbs familiar to me from my earlier visit. I noticed that more people had moved out, and that the abandoned houses appeared to lose connection with those that still had occupants. I found a sickly looking world. The neighbourhood had been cleared of silt, yet somehow these same swept streets managed to retain a memory of a mess that had been disposed of. The windows of the houses met the strong light with grudging familiarity.

Roaming dogs sniffed and crapped in the overgrown grass. For all the signs of a world getting back to its feet, such as the reconnected pylons, the abandoned houses told a different story. They seemed to suffer from a collapse of will. They looked so much smaller than those that were occupied.

I took the same route as I had months earlier, pausing near the school at the end of Eureka Street where in the autumn I had stopped to listen to the postie describe that extraordinary moment when the world had turned upside down and thrown him off his bike. Now the concrete pavements and tarred streets were as calm as a windless sea.

I crossed the road that led to Bottle Lake, with its enormous mountains of silt and piled rubble, and followed the bank beside a swollen and stinking Avon River out to Pages Road, and there, jostled by graders and trucks for space on the narrow bridge, I dropped down onto Hawke Street and continued to the sea at New Brighton.

I felt a strong need to get back out to the edge of things, to walk clear of what I had just come through.

And so, at Marine Parade, I crossed to the beach and walked on the fine sand to the water's edge, and I gazed out across the deceptively calm surface of Pegasus Bay.

Just before Christmas 2011, a series of shocks with their epicentre beneath that discreet grey lid would rock the city. We would learn it was the tailing off of seismic activity. The last hurrah—the final throat clearing of an ogre sinking into the depths of the sea.

I decided to take the track through the sandhills and walk towards South New Brighton and the sheared cliffs where houses stood split and teetering. Further around those cliffs lay Sumner.

Around the time of the school visit to the cereal factory I had come down to Sumner with Mum. We stayed at the Cave Rock Hotel. I don't remember how we travelled there. I can't imagine it would have been by plane. I would remember that. It must have been by boat, in which case the *Maori*, but I have no memory of it.

For hour after hour I was left on my own to explore the beach. The weather was much hotter than I was used to. There was also a heavy surf, and I experienced for the first time the fantastic joy of being picked up by a wave and flung back at the beach like an unwanted scrap. It was a variation of throwing myself off treetops. After collecting myself from the wet sand I ran back into the waves for more. By the end of the day, the sound of the sea was inside of my ears, and my eyelids and the tops of my ears were sunburnt. It was time to head back across the road to the Cave Rock Hotel, to trudge up the carpeted stairs in my sandy feet and count along the doors to our room, where I would find Mum, as I had left her, on the bed, staring at the ceiling. I had been gone the whole day, and for all of that time we had occupied different worlds. She was in the same state I had seen her in at home—incommunicative, a bit low, as people used to say. Of course it was the past breaking down the door. The word depression was never said aloud, and not from any sense of shame. I suspect neither Mum nor Dad would have thought it worthwhile troubling the doctor for an explanation.

~

Perhaps the cracks and fissures are carried forward. That my mother was undone by her past I have no doubt. The clues seeped from her. In her watchfulness, her eyes measured the air, always intensely aware of the climate in a room, alert to insult. Her crippling fear of rejection.

And yet, for someone like her, a victim of prejudice, oddly, she didn't hesitate to cast a few stones of her own. Some of her intolerances were generational. Swearing was one. She couldn't abide it—never swore herself. At least I never heard her. Violence was another—it disgusted her, as officially it does me too. But I also find myself helplessly drawn to its pulses. 'Man's inhumanity to man,' she'd say during yet another interminable documentary showing wartime bodies piled up, dumped in wagons and hauled across the barren wastes. I thought it profound the first time I heard her say this, but tedious thereafter, to the point where I'd fold my arms and feel my lips draw in, and find myself wishing for some cataclysmic event of man's inhumanity to man that would send bodies flying out of the television into the sitting room. One could always count on an ad break, a cup of tea and a biscuit.

It would also appear that she didn't like Catholics. And of course it would come to pass that I didn't like them either. I absorbed this prejudice as one might a family taste for a particular dish or a shared activity such as table tennis.

And so it seemed quite normal to be dismissive of our closest friends in the neighbourhood, the Browns, whose carpet I had been warned against spilling food on, as they trooped by our house each Sunday morning on their way to mass.

'There they go—off to wipe the slate clean.' I'd never heard her say anything with such forceful disdain.

I wasn't sure of what she meant the first time, but tonally it sounded as though the Browns were off to commit some disgraceful act, and therefore Mum's contempt seemed reasonable, even civically responsible, and soon I was bellowing out from the window, 'There go the Browns, off to wipe the slate clean.'

It was hardly an ecclesiastical position. We would not have known what one was, since religion was never in our sights.

But the anger rang clear—quiet, and deeply felt—not as a loud or tossed-off irritability. Now I wonder if it was the Browns' recourse to forgetting that she found so outrageously unacceptable.

~

My mother did not approve of vocal rage. It was undignified—and risky. Something might be revealed. And besides, it was not a free expression of self but a drowning, and as hopeless as the mad scrambling of a spider whirling around a plughole. She chose silence and withdrawal, and she brooded, and that was the air I grew up in, and breathed, a bruised air without any identifiable source.

Surprisingly for someone who had once sewn underclothing out of sack material for her children, Mum had a healthy sense of entitlement. I don't know where she got it from. Certainly not from Dad, who assumed whatever new pile of shit was dumped on him was all part of the world's curious design. Place them in a fairy tale, and Mum is on the winding path leading up to the palace, while Dad is heading off to the woodcutter's shed.

Perhaps her ideas of dignity and entitlement came from an alternative world she dreamt for herself. Dreams are not so easily contained or dispensed with. They cannot be taken away either.

Dreams are rarely considered as matters of heritage. But in my mother's case—perhaps in all—it would be a mistake to overlook dreams.

The kindling of revenge, but also of great deeds, and art, is forged in dreams.

As a child Tchaikovsky complained to his nanny about the noises in his head. They wouldn't let him alone at night. One of those 'noises' would turn into 'Dance of the Sugar Plum Fairy', which I first heard at primary school and then, years later, as part of an installation by Scott Eady at Te Papa Tongarewa. A tiny figure of a boxer stood on a turntable which was spun around by the tumbling motion of an agitator in an old washing machine to play the 'Sugar Plum Fairy'. Who would have thought of bringing such disparate things together? And so successfully, as it seemed to me, partly because of the memories I happened to bring to the scene. Different phrases occurred to me. Some pertinent. Others that could have come from a washing-machine manual. 'In the wash', and 'solar plexus', and 'agitator'—a vocabulary that quickly settled like compass points into familiar territory. The arbitrariness of encounter, where 'things meet in kinship', to borrow a phrase of Robert Musil's, which I had written down years earlier and which surfaced, as if on a command from long ago, in the form of the boxer and Tchaikovsky. I thought of the shore we used to pick our way along, and what we used to find there, dismembered and discarded, and flung out from the centre of human activity. And I remembered the foul weather my father walked in, without complaint, the rain filling his shoes. In similar conditions, a boilermaker-poet by the name of Hone Tuwhare felt in his back pocket for paper and a pen and wrote about holes left in the air by rain. One of these men, I am certain, felt his heart lighten.

Kindness was my father's radical response to the world. The agitator, however, has to shake the irritability out of himself somehow. For a few minutes I concentrated on the solar plexus of the washing machine, and soon enough my thoughts drifted to Bob Fitzsimmons's famous left hook to the solar plexus of Gentleman Jim Corbett. Fitzsimmons, born in Cornwall but brought up in Timaru where his heavy arms were made on a smithy's forge, was now world champion.

Later in life, Fitzsimmons meets Jack Johnson for one more

tilt at glory. By now he is an old man in boxing terms, and a bit on the light side for a heavyweight. But it is easy enough to understand what lit his candle. When does one stop dreaming? In his mind Fitzsimmons sees the fight going his way: the formidable Johnson backs up and Fitzsimmons finds room for his celebrated left hook, and relives the moment it sank into the solar plexus of Gentleman Jim Corbett all those years ago, relishing yet again the superior look sliding off Corbett's face, as if a second after the blow he too had seen the future.

In the same way that I had picked up Bob's boxing glove in the backyard and his scraps of paper with the shuffle of boxers' feet, I'd absorbed the story of Fitzsimmons' left hook to Corbett's solar plexus. Perhaps not to the extent of my brother, who would commission a bronze of the one-time blacksmith to stand on the corner of Stafford Street in Timaru, but, nevertheless, the powerful surges of ambition I experienced while taking in Scott Eady's installation were not at all of my own making, but released inside me by another layer occupied by phantoms. I must have been dreaming on Fitzsimmons' behalf.

I suppose I was taking a longer interest than most in the boxer spinning around on the turntable mounted on the washing machine. It had brought back such a flood of memories, taking me back to the washhouse air that was cool and latticed with dog hair and slow dog movement.

I was enjoying being back in the old washhouse when I became aware of the guard's breathy crossing and unfolding of his arms. We were making each other nervous. He wished what I wished—we both wished that the other would just go away. Then came a throat clearance designed to alert me to the fact that he was watching me—which of course I took quite personally—just in case, as I suspect he had it in mind, I might try to cause trouble. It hadn't occurred to me to cause trouble until then, but all of a sudden it did, and I felt a tremendous urge to smash Scott Eady's installation. The impulse came and went, leaving me in a heightened state, flushed with possibility. Of course I would never do such a thing, but mentally I had already—smashed the little fucker on the turntable playing the 'Dance of the Sugar Plum Fairy' to send him skating across the museum floor. Mentally delivering a blow is not the same as executing the action. An earthquake does not have a dress rehearsal. A car crash is not technically one until it has happened. And so Scott Eady's boxer was still campishly gliding around the turntable.

To make things worse, to inflame an already overheated situation, the guard managed a few more throat clearances. The funny thing is, eventually when I looked across to acknowledge him, I did not feel myself entirely blameless. Between the guard and me passed a separate world of cinematic scenes—in my case I saw Corbett on the canvas unable to get up and the white bony figure of Fitzsimmons turning away with the abstracted air of someone unwilling to take responsibility for the spilt milk. And as the guard nodded and I nodded back, like boxers exchanging mutual respect at the end of a particularly gruelling round, I fetched back a grainy scene from a film I barely remember except for the moment in it where the composer walks into a lake to drown himself. And instead of the violent clash that I had been gearing up for, we parted with a final nod. One from me. One from him. All perfectly civil.

~

In darkness lies the past. I will tiptoe by her closed door. The light is at the end of the hall. It is coming through the sitting room windows. I will head for the light.

~

I cannot think of a fiercer repudiation of the past than the one the ageing Krapp delivers in Samuel Beckett's play *Krapp's Last Tape*. The drawn-out silence at the beginning of the play gives no clue to the incandescent rage that erupts halfway through.

I was in an audience that waited twenty minutes for Krapp to speak. Minutes ticked by—long minutes of dream-inducing time floated through the theatre, then Krapp (played brilliantly by Michael Gambon) stood—in rancorous silence—and the heads of the audience lifted as one. Someone coughed and Gambon seemed to pause as if he had heard it, and the tension rose to an unbearable level. It would have been perfectly acceptable had someone screamed out or fainted or knifed their neighbour.

Krapp walked slowly around the desk, dragging his

knuckles against its edge. Our nerves were already jarred. Then he opened a drawer. He took out a banana, and he peeled it.

Hardly anything else happens in *Krapp's Last Tape*, and so all this time later it is the banana scene that endures—which, frankly, I could have performed just as well—but not the explosive moment when, in a furious assault on the past, Krapp turned on the tape recording of his younger self. He pulled out the tape, hurled it to the floor and stomped all over his youth and its fake eloquence.

I always used to think of myself that any eloquence I might muster was almost certainly a false wind.

What I used to like, and admire, about Beckett was his austerity. What I saw was a life pared back to its essentials. The evidence was locked in his face, in that spiky hair of his, as sturdy as a cleaning brush. I assumed he led a monastic life and existed on a diet of bread and water. In portrait after portrait his face settles into a firm jaw, the hair rears away from the scalp, and the eyes are as keen as a hawk's swooping low over a paddock. That is how I saw him, and how Beckett encouraged us to. In real life I never saw anyone quite like him. But in the imaginary landscape, he loomed—in the hacked hills and their gorse patches, and on a mad dog of a road as it twisted around corners and charged into successive stages of ugliness. I imagined Beckett's grey cosmic attention drawing up miles of tarseal on its way to some hard scrabble beach, the top button done up on his jacket, his nose flinching at the faint smell of raw sewage.

One day, idle and nosing about in a secondhand bookshop, I happened to flick through a large book of photographs taken in the south of France. Tanned 1970s women in big hair and sunglasses. Maseratis. Umbrellas, beach balls. I turned a page to find Beckett striding up a path from the beach, a towel draped over his arm, in shorts, sunglasses, sandals. It was a shock to find him in this sunny environment. I had never thought of him as a sunbather or a wearer of sandals—and of a kind similar to the brand put out by the shoe factory back in its day. But there he was, in Cap Ferrat, as I recall, the ripe smell of summer bursting from his shadow. His long tanned legs striding out. His legs were another thing to square away. His legs were beside the point. Not part of the biography.

~

The problem with my past was that all the tapes, if any ever existed, had been destroyed.

One of the few stories with an unmistakably allegorical line handed on to me had to do with hard times.

Long before you came along. Mum could always be relied on to remind me just how lucky I was to have popped up behind that cabbage leaf when I did.

Long before I came along, Bob arrived home from school to ask Mum if he could buy his school lunch like the other kids. Apparently, buying your lunch at school was a new thing, and my brother wanted to try it. But of course there was no money for such an extravagance. Bob must have kept up his campaign because eventually Mum found a few pennies behind the couch for him. He chose a pie, a meat pie (on such details memories thrive) or was it a potato pie? But come the lunch hour he couldn't eat it, and saved it instead to bring home to share.

After telling that story, Mum would nod into empty space, while I remained suitably in awe.

I might have missed it all, but I absorbed the anecdotes—the pie story and the one about Bob shooting himself—and laughed eagerly, as if I had been there, and developed a knowing smile when once more we were reminded that one sister could not be trusted to dish herself up a fair share of Spanish cream, Mum's signature dish. Strangely, this fact has endured like some oddity stuck in the sand.

Continuing with my good fortune, I didn't have to leave school at fifteen, as my sisters did, and unlike them I had a new tennis racquet and clothes bought from shops. By the age of twelve I had flown on a plane—to Sydney, then on to Surfers Paradise, where I had my first Hawaiian steak and sat speechless with joy in the holy grail of a beer garden nursing a fruit cocktail with a floating paper umbrella.

My mother dreamt of a life for herself different from the one she had landed in. She liked Englishness, good china, manners, and would often say so if someone was well spoken, but such types rarely visited 20 Stellin Street. When they did, we sat around in a circle like newly minted disciples. The one who could talk—and very persuasively—was my brother.

He did not so much smash as talk his way out of our working-class stocks, which was to make the way a great deal easier for me. I was lucky enough to attend university—not that I intended to, but he insisted. And because of Bob's success in commercial property, Dad was able to retire from welding. Mum, who had cleaned houses to supplement the household income and sewn underpants for her kids, would fly first-class for the rest of her life, and once, memorably, in a chartered jet all around Australia. And because she could now afford to she shook the lines of depression and disappointment out of her face. For the last thirty years of her life, she took an anti-depressant pill every day. The effect was extraordinary. It seemed to strip away the protective layers to allow a different person to emerge—a far more cheerful person. It was not a mask she put on before our startled eyes but a part of her that had lain buried for so long without the means to emerge and express itself. She turned into a lovely old lady whose welcoming hug at the door and demand for a peck on her cheek suddenly felt weirdly inappropriate, even unsettling. I wasn't used to this person, and if I could I would step around her and brush aside her protests. To be met at the door by all that charm and lipstick—it was too much. It was as if someone else who was only vaguely familiar had taken up residence inside her. Whenever I indulged her it felt like we were playing at something, like grappling with a foreign language, or acting out roles in a play for which we had only some of the lines.

Just as annoying, some old habits remained. She would yell

at me as I reached for a piece of fruit in the bowl. She had *just* bought those bananas. What on earth made me think I could eat one? A week later, the bananas would still be there, soft, untouched, and covered in black spots.

Such moments might have been an act of solidarity with the single mums she taught to budget, something she knew quite a bit about, even though these days she drove a late-model Jaguar to the Citizens Advice Bureau in the Hutt to give advice to desperate young women arriving on the bus.

~

I am made aware of how the world is built from what lies near to hand. A musical instrument can be made by stringing sheep gut between two goat horns. And fate can intervene in surprising ways. Whoever would have thought of giving a flying ram to a nymph in order for her to rescue her children from a murderous father? Or to cast a spell over guard dogs and to steal their bark? And I know how theft can be a kind of comic correction to the world order, such as when stolen cattle are made to walk backwards to throw off their pursuers. Although, in the account of the myth I prefer, brushes are tied to the tails of the cattle bringing up the rear to erase all trace of their passing. I also understand that vengeance knows no restraint. Rulers are turned into ravens, their children into twittering birds, and betrayers into stone.

I know all about Hermes because 'for the sake of my

education' Mum has taken out a subscription to *Knowledge* magazine, which now regularly turns up in the letterbox at 20 Stellin Street.

I've also read that Hermes, the interpreter of dreams and messenger of the gods, bestowed on the witness Aesop the gift of fable.

As it happens, I have a real-life magician in my life capable of spinning gold out of air.

Each Sunday, Bob comes home for the roast.

He parks his fabulously expensive sports car in the drive by the rubbish bins, which attracts the neighbourhood kids and dogs. He is often too excited to eat. Instead he paces up and down the small kitchen recounting adventures to do with his salesmen who sell advertising space to tradesmen in something called *The Bride Book*.

My brother brings into that tiny kitchen a life brimming with wild and outrageous stories. He is often at the heart of them. For diversion there is the map of the world pinned to the wall. My father keeps his head down and tucks solitarily into his meat and potatoes. It's almost as if he can't hear. On the other hand, he will sometimes remember me and before his mouth closes down on a forkful of meat call out across the table, 'Capital of China?'

Bob's stories have a touch of Robin Hood about them. Mum might smile, or catch herself to turn the smile into a look of official disapproval. Perhaps it is because the world that my brother brings to our attention has such different rules. As far as

I can tell, there aren't any. It's a world in which Henry Fielding's foundling bastard Tom Jones would flourish. In many ways, Tom Jones belongs in our family tree, along with Hermes. And here, too, a lesson was to be absorbed as completely as I had absorbed the pie story and less honourably Mum's anti-Catholicism. You could be anyone and achieve anything. Secondly, 'work' was a loose and imaginative word. Our father had flogged himself half to death for nothing. From now on things would be different. My brother had found a way.

It was the 1960s, and huge tracts of the planet we are familiar with today—South America, to choose but one continent—did not register in any other way than on the map. In the world beyond the rubbish bins a young couple fell in love, got engaged, bought a section, and got cracking with building a house. Ideally the last nail was banged in as she dropped her first kid.

As corny as it sounds now, *The Bride Book* spoke of happier times ahead. Not so much for the couples. The business model behind *The Bride Book* didn't really give a toss about them. No—happier times for the tradesmen, and the enormous business opportunities associated with a couple's decision to get hitched, usually after the first fumbling in the back seat of a car parked down by the river.

A plumber or an electrician or a marriage celebrant, tilers and specialists in linoleum and lights and fittings—none of them could afford to miss out. Hermes could not have done better to come up with *The Bride Book* to exploit the standard fairy tale so irresistible from the beginning of time. The wonderful irony is that its creator came from a family riven with illegitimacy and abandonment.

The world beyond the rubbish bins, I understand, is a pantomime. Someone is always pretending to be someone they're not. The men who work for Bob have nicknames like 'Twelve Foot'. Like all extremely tall men, Twelve Foot came through the door with a bowed head and stayed like that after he sat down at the dinner table to tuck into Mum's roast. Mr Moses was another pseudonym I heard, entirely appropriate for someone offering the Promised Land to a dazzled builder caught halfway up a ladder. And Rick, of course, who my mother objected to because, she said, he was good-looking. She also objected to his teeth, which, as far as I could see, were perfect. The smile and its flashing white teeth went into overdrive whenever he entered the kitchen. Mum would look away grimly. And Rick was canny enough to know to address Mum as Mrs Jones, never Joyce.

In the late 1960s Bob handed on *The Bride Book* to Lorraine's husband Michael, who continued to run it from its Hutt offices on the street behind the riverbank.

After school I would pop in there to stuff calendars covered in trade ads into tubes.

Through the open office door I listened to Michael rehearse a new salesman. And it was like catching up with a story first heard around the Sunday roast years earlier. 'Now, I will be Mr Brown. You be Mr Green.'

The trainee salesman would leave the office to compose himself as Mr Green. He barely noticed the kid in the corner stuffing tubes. But I noticed him, and a whole swag of other Mr Greens in their badly ironed white shirts and skinny black ties, each one with a face like a Mormon's, young, spotty, lips mumbling the lines that would take him out to the world as Mr Green. He took a deep breath and disappeared around the office door. 'Hello Mr Brown. I'm Mr Green…' followed a few moments later by howls of laughter.

'From Rags to Riches.' I was nine or ten when I saw that headline. I remember the thrill of seeing Lorraine, then just a few years out of living in a caravan in the Hutt Park campground, photographed by the newspaper—there she was, in the paper, holding a model of a commercial building in Andrews Avenue, which on completion would become the tallest building in the Hutt, and owned by my brother.

Bob had become a millionaire, once upon a time a thing unimaginable to the inhabitants at 20 Stellin Street. But, at a deeper level, nothing much else was to change. The history that went untold was still manifestly present—in Dad's struggle to make himself understood, in Mum's neurosis.

In my own case, it was in an outsider's feel for the margins, and a contempt for anyone who might think themselves part of the establishment, while, paradoxically, not necessarily condemning the idea of the establishment. One can still admire the crystal without feeling a need to own it. Pretension was the offending character trait.

It never occurred to me that my heritage also included a rich lineage of jesters and fools and risk-takers who could be depended upon to say aloud what everyone else thought but could not bring themselves to say.

But it also came with a recklessness. Words could lead you anywhere. It was just a matter of trusting them completely.

~

There was a time when I pursued my wife's family lore all the way to the Ukraine. It didn't seem such a crazy idea to seek out the source of a physical similarity between my eldest son and his great-grandfather. I did sometimes wonder if Jo's grandfather really had been a violinist to the Czar, but there was his portrait in such proximity to our own lives, overseeing the scamper and hijinks of kids running up and down the hall, returning my own gaze with equanimity, as though he guessed my doubts and wished to reassure me that, yes, everything I'd heard was true.

This was big history, desirable history—and it happened in places that I wanted to visit. One year I travelled to Moldova, well outside the 'family map', and, being short of leads, I found myself inventing one. I said whatever needed to be said to persuade the Moldovan Embassy in Moscow to give me a visa, which is how I came to find myself sitting in a hotel room in Kishinev with a map open on my knees and a cross marked on Zura, a tiny village on the banks of the Dniester which tumbles down from the top of Russia to the Black Sea.

I liked the sound of Zura. It was so out of the way and unreachable that the only legitimate excuse to visit was to invent a family history that included Zura. I'd told the consul that my wife's ancestor had floated down the Dniester until he reached Zura. And when did this happen? I could offer only approximate dates.

It seems preposterous now, but I remember calmly describing this piece of family history with the sangfroid of a salesman for *The Bride Book* or, for that matter, Arthur Leonard Jones inventing his drowned-at-sea story.

Otherwise Zura was a world that I would never have found. And, with some justification, grandfather Arthur Leonard Jones might claim that with the drowned-at-sea story he would never have found his third wife and, for all I know, happiness.

My interpreter was an out-of-work schoolteacher in Kishinev. Her boyfriend, an agricultural inspector, happened to know Zura; he drove there a few times a month. His tiny car was a familiar sight to the soldiers at the roadblocks at each bridge, and so we were waved through. There was a war on. Or one had just finished. A few weeks earlier we'd have been in Moldova. Now the border had moved and we were driving through Western Dniester. Eventually we came to Zura, a small village of unsealed roads. Across the river was Romania.

Without the thread of make-believe, I would never have met the old Jewish man. A crowd gathered around the cherry tree where I sat with the mayor and the interpreter and the agricultural inspector while we waited for the old man to turn up to shed light on my wife's ancestors.

He duly arrived with a small briefcase much like the one Dad used to carry his sandwiches and tobacco in to the factory where he made fire engines.

Short, thin, weak-kneed, dressed for the occasion in a threadbare suit and a frayed shirt collar. Bits of newspaper flopped out the sides of his cracked shoes. His eyes were large and still, and never once blinked. His face was sparsely covered in grey stubble.

A chair was found for him. He was treated with much respect, which he took in his stride, or, as it later occurred to me, dismissed as too little and too late. He shook his head at the offer of a drink from a jug of cold red wine. His eyes tended to weep, and he kept dabbing at them with an old rag.

The air was cool out of the sun and where we sat under the tree was in partial shadow. I picked at the cherries and spat the stones onto the ground as I had seen the mayor do.

The old man set his briefcase on the table. Inside it were news clippings from the war. As they were written in Russian I handed them to the interpreter. A small crowd stood behind us. The interpreter put on her glasses. I could hear the river tinkling between the small houses. A car slowed down for a look, then drove on.

As the interpreter began to read the old man came to life. Every now and then he nodded at something she said, and when she ended he announced grandly that after he was drafted into the Soviet Army he had fought on every front. I remembered the evenings in front of the telly, the carts piled with bodies and the landscapes stitched with barbed wire, and, heard again Mum's lament about man's inhumanity to man.

His voice was surprisingly emphatic, like Mum's at the end of her life when she seemed briefly to recover her voice, but not her control, so that her words came out in different registers, surprising too like an unexpected burp, and I remember thinking at the time that it was as though she was emptying the bilges of all the lives she had lived, one moment sounding like a little girl, harsh and guttural in the next, and then a scolding sound that was emphatic, such as her reprimand when I had reached for a banana; the old man in Zura sounded the same way as he stabbed the air with his finger and listed all the fronts he had fought on.

The crowd listened and nodded silently like a cast of extras, but now he was repeating himself and they waited patiently for something new. I endeavoured to look like I was listening hard before becoming distracted by the old man's whiskers, noting again how distinct and sparse they were.

In the Soviet Army the old man had had countless brushes with death—his body was covered with shrapnel wounds—but being drafted undoubtedly saved his life. At the end of the war he made his way back to Zura to discover he had fought in a losing war after all. The Romanians had thrown every last Jew into the river, including all the members of his family.

The old man leant towards the interpreter and in a hoarse voice muttered at length. 'Yes,' she said. And, looking around for me, she added, 'He is the last one left.'

No one spoke while the old man closed his briefcase and stood to leave. No one moved as he made his way out the gate. The interpreter took hold of my arm. 'Any relative of your wife,' she said, 'almost certainly drowned in the river.'

~

I had taken to travel at quite a young age, thinking that if I moved through the world with my mouth, ears and eyes open, something would catch. And it did, fleetingly. The world flooded in through the windows of buses and trains across America and Europe. And at odd times a picture of Dad would slide into view—of him at the kitchen sink, gazing out through the window to the street with his ship-rail stare. And always it was a disappointing place to arrive back to, one that I had fled from because it seemed to locate me, as well as define me. And I didn't wish for either.

But that winter, as I wandered through zones of dereliction in Christchurch, I was being nudged quietly homewards on currents I was hardly aware of.

The air in the city was thin, it almost hurt to breathe, and a week-old snow stuck around. I found myself outside the basilica staring through the barrier at the autumnal bronze leaves of a hornbeam tree. I was told the leaves would hold on until the spring growth began to come through. The tenacity of the hornbeam stood in stark contrast to everything crumbling around it. It would hang on until it didn't need to. Things, it seems, had first to set, then unravel, for the new growth to begin. In this way old information had a way of becoming new information.

FIVE

IN MY MOTHER'S memory things just happened. Big life-shattering breaches went unexplained or were distilled down to a Punch and Judy line: *Well, she had to choose between him and me, and in the end she chose him.*

But things don't ever just happen. Things occur in a particular way and for a reason.

Mum never did see inside the folder held in the vaults of the national archives. Here, the past was presented with disarming bureaucratic plainness—a brown folder bound with packaging string. In late 2011, it sat before me on a reader's desk. For a few minutes I did little more than stare at it. Then, slowed down by a ceremonial sense of how to proceed, I pulled gently on the ends of the string, and the folder breathed out. And I smelt the old air of an unvisited room shut up for the better part of a century.

It was like the end of a long flight when you wake in time for the descent through the cloud and look out the window to the startling detail of a place you have only vaguely heard about. And because the detail has a fresh and unclaimed quality, the fevered eye seeks out everything all at once.

That is what happened with my first reading of the 125-page court transcript of Maud's divorce from Harry Nash. I read quickly in order to reach the end, then I went back to the beginning and read everything more carefully. It was the third or fourth reading before various details found one another. Inevitably, a narrative began to take shape. I began to see Maud. And, rather wonderfully, a grandfather whom I never knew, emerged—my mother's father, a farmer from North Canterbury. I read with a jurist's attention. I read with glee, and I read with a next-of-kin's cringing sense of embarrassment. Opinions formed and shifted. I read with an open mind, which led to a sympathy for someone for whom I'd only ever felt contempt. And then I read with imagination in order to bring to the surface the motivations that the jury apparently could not see for itself, and I read in such a way that I found myself reconsidering everything that I'd known about my grandmother, Maud.

The pity is my mother never got to hear Maud tell her own story, or to hear what her own mother had had to say about her.

～

Now there were dates, departures, places, occupations to consider. The positioning of a life in Somerset followed by upheaval. And, of course, the 'facts', such as they are.

Maud was an assistant mistress of a 'high school' in Wellington, Somerset, where she spent seven years looking after 'the little ones' (receiving 'a certificate for efficiency').

In 1912, aged twenty-eight, she worked her passage as the governess to the children of a headmaster and his wife and sailed out to New Zealand. As the court transcript doesn't mention this fact, I have an idea Mavis told me. I have a faint recollection of her describing a general uprooting of the family around that time to various places across the globe. Canada was mentioned, and a number of American cities. Chicago, I seem to recall.

A brother, Bert, who surfaces during the divorce trial, said his sister came out to New Zealand in order to 'better herself'. But look at what she left behind.

I type 'Wellington Somerset 1912' into my browser and discover a very pleasant English market town. Ivy, hedges, canvas awnings shading a line of shops. People on foot share a thinly populated road with a few figures on large bicycles and a horse and carriage. In their caps and heavy black footwear three boys in a market street look like miniature adults. There is a monument on a hill and a public garden, much like any to be found in Christchurch or Wellington at that time: flax, a cabbage tree, cypress trees, paths, a sweep of lawn. A steady sky, a wisp of cloud. There is a tranquillity not easily found in the landscape that Maud arrives to.

The slopes of the Rimutakas that rise like the gates to a forbidden kingdom at the head of the Hutt Valley have been relentlessly logged. In the city of Wellington a deforested Mt Victoria looms above dwellings of corrugated iron and unpainted timber like a giant mudslide waiting to happen. From the wharves the bare hills look hobbled and barnacled with small timber cottages. It is as though the original builders set off with a wheelbarrow and spade, and a tool to hack their way through the bush, with instructions to pitch their tent wherever they saw fit. If Maud's eye for efficiency took in all of this, she will have noted that roads do not rule these hills. It is hill first, then outlook and aspect, then the house itself, and finally the road, which is a glorified term for a track pitching in and out of ferny shadow to sun-lit bends walloped by the wind. The same wind that threatened to lift me off the tops of Pencarrow as a small boy shakes the living daylights out of anything not pegged or anchored down. The bonnets in the market street of Wellington, Somerset, would not last a second.

Why did she settle here, in the wind-blasted Wellington down under? For my mother's sake. I'll come to that.

Maud leaves the headmaster and his wife in the capital and continues to Christchurch to stay 'with friends'. Who are these friends? No names are given. They live on a farm 'in the South Island', which again is not very exact. Maud is there a year. Then, towards the end of 1913, she takes a position on a North Canterbury sheep farm, where for another year, she says, 'I acted as a housekeeper'.

If she came up from Christchurch, she would have taken a train to the small North Canterbury township of Hawarden, and from there driven by horse and buggy to Taruna, the sheep farm of Owen Tibbott (O.T.) Evans.

~

I have always thought of Maud as old. Her name makes her old to start with. And being my mother's mother makes her older still.

I have to remind myself that this traveller is a young woman. In Taruna, she is a young woman with barely a neighbour for miles around. There are the mountains at the back of the house. Sheep in the paddocks provide small shifts in the landscape. The wind from the nor-west is like some incessant curse whistling in the eaves when she is heating water, hissing in her ear when she is pegging up the washing. It is there in her face, in her hair, whenever she walks down the long drive to stand by the letter-box. But then, without warning, come moments of absolute stillness, and it is as if the world is telling her, 'Look where you have arrived. You have fallen through a hole in the earth.' Of course I am imposing my own thoughts on Maud. She may have felt differently. Taruna with its majestic setting may have seemed like the start of something new.

The court transcript has very little to say about Maud's time at Taruna. But it is here that she became pregnant to O.T.

As far as the court record is concerned, Taruna is just a

prelude. But it interests me. There is the figure of a grandfather to disinter. There is a romance to imagine. Leading up to and during the time my mother was conceived, O.T.'s wife, Maggie, was staying at their Christchurch residence, nursing their first-born, Geoffrey. My mother was born in December 1914, but as late as May of that year Maud is still in the district. Her name appears in the Christchurch *Press* along with a number of other women who ran a clothing stall that month to raise funds for the tennis courts and bowling green in Waipara, the nearest town.

So, clearly, she is part of the community, pitching in. She is already two months pregnant when she helps out at the stall. People will know her—perhaps by name. At the very least they have seen her face around.

Perhaps she doesn't yet know she is pregnant—but the moment of discovery cannot be far off.

If Maud's world is about to gain another dimension, O.T. must have felt as though his was teetering. It is also clear that Maud's family in England never knew about the pregnancy. The decision to keep it a secret was taken early. One imagines the conversations, difficult conversations long into the night, about what to do. In 1914, a child born out of wedlock was occasion for tremendous shame. The Salvation Army gathered at the bottom of the cliff with its various categories of 'fall' to consider—*how long fallen, first fallen, twice fallen,* and so on. The method of fall had its particulars—*taken advantage of, alcohol, foolishly led astray, bad company, seduced, ruined under the promise of marriage.* A high percentage of 'fallen women' in the care of the Salvation Army Home were domestic servants, often from humble origins.

Nathaniel Hawthorne's story of a fallen woman in *The Scarlet Letter* brought him fame on both sides of the Atlantic. For a time the novelist was the American consul in Liverpool, a role that his wife excitedly wrote is second in importance only to the embassy in London. In Liverpool, Hawthorne liked to roam the docks. One day he stopped to observe a procession of girls and young women from the workhouse heading to the dock to board the ship that would take them out to the new world to work as domestic servants. He wrote in *English Notebooks*:

> I should not have conceived it possible that so many children could have been collected together, without a single trace of beauty or scarcely of intelligence in so much as one individual...[their] coarse, vulgar features and figures betraying unmistakably low origin, and ignorant and brutal parents. They did not appear wicked, but only stupid, and animal and soulless.

The *Asia*, with the Bibbys on board, had stopped in Ireland to pick up a number of women from the workhouse to deliver to Port Chalmers in New Zealand, where most of them, according to a follow-up report, proved themselves to be entirely useless as domestic servants. A small number were held in barracks from where they were in the habit of escaping, getting drunk, and coming into quick money in 'unexplained ways'.

If Hawthorne's notebook entry speaks of type, in *The Scarlet Letter* we find a more sympathetic portrayal of the fallen woman in the form of Hester Prynne.

As in a Puritan village in Massachusetts, so in a colony emerging from the Victorian era at the bottom of the Pacific, a child born out of wedlock was a life-shattering event. The shame had to be absorbed until the fall became part of the life story, shaping all those touched by it.

The catastrophe for fallen women such as Maud and Hester is the length of the fall. Both women will go on breaking their fall with one hand while clinging onto their child with the other.

My mother's story begins here—with her own mother in flight.

~

How fiercely present the world is.

How nice and orderly its arrangement.

Through the trees the glinting paddocks and their bright promise. The road that brought Maud here now leads her discreetly away.

This is the last time she will set eyes on Taruna. And then she is on a train, on her way out of the farmer's world. An overnight ferry pushes by the mountainous Kaikoura coast and on to the windswept strait.

Until the baby arrives there is not much to do other than wait in Wellington, perhaps grow bored with the hospital window and its cloudless day. It is coming into summer.

Maud's confinement is spent in a private hospital. Later she will tell the court that she paid for this herself—clearly a matter of personal satisfaction to her. But which hospital? I wonder if it was Calvary where I had my tonsils out when I was eleven. Nuns, the first I had ever seen, had glided along its corridors. Or St Helen's, a specialist maternity hospital on Coromandel Street that climbs up from the Newtown shops on Adelaide Road. But that maternity hospital was for married women.

She may have snuck in there. Funny to think of Maud's recourse to invention beginning with her admission to a maternity hospital.

There were options—abortion, adoption, infanticide. But Maud's mind is made up, if indeed there was any doubt. The bathroom mirror holds her gaze and reports back the ordinary truth of someone looking for something that is not there. She is pregnant with a child. She hasn't robbed a bank.

She will keep my mother. But to do so will require another sacrifice. She decides to drop out of sight, to self-erase.

She stops writing to friends and family in England. She will end all communication with the people who knew her before she entered hospital.

By the time she has given birth to my mother, Maud has accomplished something similar for herself—she has a new name, a whole new identity. She has created a widow's story for herself.

She is now May Seaward. Maud has an aunt by that name from Portsmouth. She will say May is from Portsmouth as well, and since she must give an occupation to 'the late Mr Seaward', he can be an engineer, someone able and essential to the creation of new worlds.

A man named Harry Nash has advertised in the local newspaper for a live-in housekeeper. In her letter of application Maud says she is after such a position with a 'refined family who would not object to her and her little girl'. When Nash replies that the position has been taken, Maud writes back, 'I was sorry not to have got the position of housekeeper to you, but would be pleased if at a future time you are unsuited you would write to me.'

The letter is on file; her forwarding address is care of a Mrs Harrison, Rodrigo Road, Kilbirnie. Who is Mrs Harrison? We hear no more of her.

Maud finds another live-in position, this one on a farm in Gladstone in the Wairarapa, 130 kilometres from Wellington. The Tararuas, which divide the Wairarapa from the Manawatu in the west, are not nearly as imposing as the Southern Alps, but they offer the same feeling of wilderness at the end of the road. Maungahuia, which is the name of the farm, and locality, sits inside a bowl of cleared hills, where the grasslands are still coming into being. The summer air is filled with thick smoke. Ash drifts across the farm—it gathers along the windowsills, and marks the lines of washed sheets.

On summer nights, people drive to the edge of the burn off to take in the spectacle. Buggies and drays by the dozen, one or two cars, a truck, and in the dark the awe-struck crowd gazes up at a sky that burns like a fabulous city. Bright embers fill the night and as one dies another takes its place. High above the lit sky is another, larger chamber containing the galaxy that is permanent and glowing.

Weeks later, by which time the lit sky has drifted down to earth, the blackened stumps smoulder into the grey hour. Shouting men call their dogs back from the burning ash. Within a year or two no one will remember what was there. A cow will graze on grass where once stood a three-hundred-year-old tree. And a dreadful silence rolls out where once the distinctive call of the huia was heard through the forested slopes. Women liked to wear the huia beak as a brooch and its distinctive white-tipped tail feathers made an attractive adornment. Now, the only huia left are stuffed and mounted. When I was a child the bird still graced a sixpenny postage stamp. And I have heard it said that it derived its name from a distress call—*uia, uia, uia*, or (in Maori) Where are you?

Maungahuia, 'the hill of the huia', can be seen on a country road before Gladstone. The original farmstead where Maud and my mother stayed has gone, and the forest that covered the hill of the huia has disappeared. The farmer of a farmhouse I visited believes the last huia was found lying dead on a tennis court around the time of the First World War.

The spell in hospital must have made a favourable impression, possibly it was the nurses who moved swiftly and unseeing, because within a few months of moving to isolated Maungahuia, Maud has decided she would like to become a nurse. She writes to St Helen's Hospital, the maternity hospital for married mothers, and receives notice that a new intake won't be accepted until September 1915. Meanwhile, a letter from Harry Nash arrives to say that the position in his household has become free. Maud replies that she can offer him six months until the hospital intake later in the year. Nash writes back with his acceptance.

~

In late February 1915, armed with their invented histories, Maud and my mother enter the household of Harry Nash on Upland Road.

The widow and widower ought to have this much in common—the persistent shadow of the absent spouse, and the confusion thrown up by a suddenly lopsided life.

Everywhere inside the house are photographs of the late Mrs Nash. Maud, of course, has none to show of the late Mr Seaward. And Mr Nash has three children, two sons and a daughter, all of them at boarding school. Their faces are easily traced back to the photograph of the late Mrs Nash. But when Harry Nash studies my mother, her lineage is not so easily pinned down. Perhaps there is something of Maud's long face, and her pale blue eyes, but then the terrain mysteriously changes into the features of the farmer who cannot be named.

Mr Seaward, on the other hand, can be anyone. For a number of months Maud keeps her widow's story afloat. There is a lot at stake. She has landed on her feet—she has comfort and a degree of security in Nash's house. Kelburn is an attractive neighbourhood on the fringe of the city. Upland Road winds through a muddle of small hills and valleys. There are plunging views over orange-tiled roofs. But it is difficult terrain for a pram. Maud has to push and shove uphill and then grip the pram going down to prevent my mother from rolling away.

Harry Nash has proposed, and after only three weeks of Maud and my mother moving in. Maud has asked for a day to think it over. Obviously she has slept with Nash. It is easy to work out since her first child to Nash, Eric, is born that year in December, barely nine months after she and my mother arrived from Gladstone.

Quite coincidentally, as Maud would have it, she bumps into O.T. Evans on Lambton Quay in the city. She told the court that the farmer was on his way to Porirua, then farmland, now covered in state housing. O.T. might have come up to Wellington on business. It is possible. But so might have been a planned visit to see Maud and my mother.

In Maud's account she tells the farmer she is to marry. The farmer is pleased. She doesn't mention 'relieved'.

More significantly, Harry Nash has offered to adopt my

mother, to bring her up as 'one of his own', and in the end that's what persuades Maud to accept his marriage offer, in order, she told the court, to give 'Betty a name'.

~

Betty. It is there in the transcript. After knowing her all my life as Joyce, it is weirdly dislocating—even euphonically jarring—to discover Mum is in fact Betty.

For the first years of her life she is Betty—Betty Seaward with a false past and a father who doesn't exist.

Betty is a complete stranger to me. Betty suggests someone ready with a tray of cakes in the unexpected delight of visitors turning up to the door. Betty suggests an open smile. My mother's smile was more guarded and, before the happy pills took effect, only ever parsimoniously wheeled out. Although on the odd occasion it could blossom with indecent delight, such as when she was reminded that her careless driving had knocked a boy off his bike and she replied, 'Oh, you mean that *fat* boy!'

She was Betty until the age of four—long enough for the cast of personality to set around that name. And yet, try as I may, I can't recall a time when that first name floated to the surface. Is it possible for a name to just fade away?

While that may be so, the larger world inhabited by Betty stayed with her, because Betty, it turns out, belongs to a household of verbal and physical abuse, humiliation, threats, and endless push-and-shove violence between Maud and Harry that, on occasion, rose to madness.

~

On 29 June 1915, Maud and Harry Nash marry in the Presbyterian manse in Ellice Street, Mt Victoria.

Before the wedding Maud makes a terrible mistake. She decides she will tell Harry the truth. There is no Mr Seaward. There was never any engineer. She is not a widow. She made it all up, but it was a necessary tale, because otherwise she would be a single woman with a child in tow, a social pariah, like Hawthorne's Hester Prynne and her daughter Pearl, each a liability to the other.

A resentful Nash feels he has been doubly deceived—first, by Maud's lies, and second, by the timing of her confession. The invitations have already gone out. It is too late to recant and cancel the wedding.

A different question now occurs to Nash. If there is no Mr Seaward, then who is the father of the child?

Maud will not say.

~

Nor would Hester Prynne as she stood on a scaffold with her child before a hostile crowd, facing down a clergyman's insistence that she name 'him who tempted you to this grievous fall'.

'Speak and give your child a name,' demands a voice in the crowd below the scaffold.

'Never,' she replies.

She is further condemned for her obstinacy and reminded of 'the vileness and blackness' of her sin.

The scene shifts to a courthouse where an old minister is instructed to examine Pearl for the Christian qualities as would befit a child of her age. Pearl escapes through an open window to stand on an outside step 'looking like a wild tropical bird of rich plumage, ready to take flight into the upper air'. Peering out the window the old man asks, 'Who made thee?' Pearl sticks her finger in her mouth to consider the question. She announces she was not made at all, but (in a variation of my own cabbage-patch origins) was 'plucked by her mother off the bush of wild roses that grew by the prison door'.

In frustration the magistrate turns to the physician who undertakes to analyse the child's nature and 'from its make and mould, to give a shrewd guess at the father'.

~

Maud's refusal to name my mother's father enrages Nash. Someone has got away with something for which he must pay. He stomps about with moral indignation. But, I wonder, is that what really galls him? Or is it Maud's evasiveness on the subject of the father, the fact that she will not reveal the man's name or say anything bad about him? If she won't, then he will—and he ends up feeling foolish for slandering a ghost.

What does her silence mean? He turns his attention to Betty. She is someone else's love child. He is the sop who picks up the bills. He lifts her up and tries to shake her father's name out of her. She doesn't understand, of course, that she is a meteorite that has crashed into Nash's world or that what he holds in his hands is not just a child, but evidence of Maud's alternative object of affection.

Over the coming months Nash comes up with a formula designed to satisfy him and make Maud miserable. She must be made to understand that the world will not bend to her will. She cannot have the child and also expect to have him, not after the exposure of Mr Seaward as a fabrication. If she won't reveal the identity of the father, Maud must choose between Nash and her daughter.

—

It is easy to see where Eric and Ken have sprung from. Harry can find plenty in them that is reassuringly familiar. He is present, and so is Maud. But the man Maud won't name is also present—in my mother's face, inside Harry's house, sitting up to the table, almost one of them.

Nash takes to bullying and humiliating mother and child in public.

By now, Mum and the Nashs are living in Manley Terrace, Newtown, and it is here that things spiral into violence.

One afternoon Maud comes home to find my mother bleeding from the face. Harry says the child cut her nose on the bars of the cot as he was lifting her out. Maud looks at the blood on the floor, and at my mother, and accuses Nash of striking her. Infuriated at having his word questioned, Nash raises his hand to hit her, whereupon Maud runs into the kitchen for the carving knife.

What the neighbours see is Harry Nash backing out of the house onto the street and Maud in the doorway holding the knife.

Some weeks later, the same neighbours witness Maud hanging out of an upstairs window. Two male hands grip her.

Whose hands are they? Harry Nash's? Who else could they belong to? In which case, are those hands trying to save Maud? But from what—self-harm? Or are they threatening to drop her out the window?

The neighbours rush inside the house and pound up the stairs to find Maud on the bed, exhausted, with a black eye and red marks on her face.

The same neighbours report rows at night—Harry playing his piano ever louder, Maud retaliating on her violin, scratching her notes, sawing into Nash's brain; Nash violently crashing his hands down on the piano keys. On it goes until the neighbours call the police. On their arrival, the transformation in Harry Nash is remarkable. He is suddenly calm, thoughtful, concerned.

~

By the time I enter the world the stain has spread. Maud is callous and dreadful and manipulative. But no one had bothered to wonder why.

In 1923 separation and divorce were the business of the court, and anyone willing to go through the ordeal had to face a jury, like a criminal, and the prospect of their dirty washing hung out for all to see.

For Maud, the courtroom has turned itself into a version of the scaffold on which Hawthorne's Hester Prynne was made to stand with her daughter Pearl and atone for her sins.

Nash's case is based on proving that Maud is guilty of mental cruelty towards him. Maud denies the charge, and for her own reasons is just as eager to prove that Nash is guilty of cruelty towards her with physical and verbal abuse of her and her child. And worse—blackmail, which is how the name of O.T. Evans surfaces, although his name never makes it into the newspaper coverage of the trial.

I read the letters between Maud and O.T., then returned to the court transcript. I picked up the letters. I read them more carefully a second and third and fourth time. I went back to the transcript. I didn't know what to think or whose word to take. Maud is as mad as a snake. Nash is a violent man. The transcript is infuriatingly inconclusive. However, the tinder and flames that produced the long smouldering silence that hovered over my childhood are there.

My mother was present all those times Maud and Nash traded blows. She was there when Nash dragged her mother about the house and jumped on her stomach. She was upstairs in the house in Manley Terrace when Nash attempted to throw her mother out the top-floor window. She was definitely there when Nash followed mother and daughter through the streets of Newtown shouting indignantly—as if from some bizarre local remake of *The Scarlet Letter*—that the child there is a bastard child!

By today's standards, such a charge is absurd. But the charge doesn't matter as much as the shame of having it yelled in the street, and shame is toxic.

Perhaps after a while these humiliations turned into the distant rumble of passing thunder. I imagine Mum was too young to know that the argument in that marriage was all about her, and that the lies Maud told were to protect her and her father.

Seeing everything so plainly set out, the 'facts' or, I should say, the nakedness of the facts—I didn't expect to feel the revulsion that came over me.

A woman who is my grandmother, a stranger up to this point, suddenly appears before me—on the page—waving a carving knife in her husband's face. It was embarrassing to meet her first up like this. I even felt oddly implicated—she is my grandmother after all. We may not have set eyes on one another but she is partly responsible for the genes spilling around inside me, and so I found myself looking for and finding traces of self-recognition, not so much in the violence—apart from her attack on Nash's piano with an axe (I once took an axe to a blow heater which had exacerbated my hayfever)—but in her persistence and the quiet indignation that sat behind it.

I read on. Maud throws filthy nappies in Nash's face. She aims a heavy enamel billy at him but instead strikes new baby Eric on the head. Nash dashes from the house with the baby in his arms thinking it is dead. Maud attacks Nash with a carving knife as he sits down to breakfast. She threatens to kill Nash, and attacks him with a towel-rack. The following day she chases him from the house with a table knife. She repeatedly insults Nash in front of his customers and staff, calling him a liar and 'the son of a convict'—the unfortunate Nash was born in Melbourne—possibly in retaliation for Nash calling her 'the mother of all lies'. She hurls an electric iron at him; attacks him with scissors; smashes a window in a fit of ill-temper; scratches his face, disfiguring him; kicks him in the groin while he is cutting the hedge and forcing him to his bed for a week. Soon after that, she flies at Nash with a pair of scissors. She sets fire to Nash's walking stick. 'In a fit of rage' she smashes a window with a clothes brush.

After a lifetime of hardly knowing a thing about Maud, suddenly there's too much. She is not the person I took her to be. She is worse.

Once more I make myself reread everything in the court transcript, and this time I decide differently. She is a quiet woman who, nonetheless, happens to be armed with a carving knife. She is a schoolteacher, a woman with blue eyes and blonde hair seeking a 'refined home for herself and her little girl' who, nonetheless, happens to be armed with a carving knife.

Why?

Harry Nash has applied to the court for a Decree of Separation. He is the petitioner; Maud is the respondent. In the language of the law Maud is charged with having

> pursued a course of conduct calculated to break down [Nash's] spirit and to cause his health to break down, [Maud] having constantly heaped abuse upon [Nash], having frequently assaulted [Nash] and his children by a previous marriage, and having attempted to humiliate [Nash] before his employees and customers.

Nash's evidence must fit the charge. As the petitioner he also has first say. Maud's violence appears indefensible. But deeper into the transcript the picture changes. I found myself taking a more sympathetic view.

More so than the grub covering the trial as a newspaper artist for *Truth*. Under a headline 'The Little Pugilist' he has lengthened Maud's profile in order to give her a hooked nose and joyfully made her unflattering hat even more outlandish to crown his obvious hope of conjuring up a witch. His treatment of Harry Nash is more respectful. Harry appears in a suit with collar and tie; he is business-like in bearing. He looks dependable rather than sharp. No part of him comes in for lampooning, although his moustache is possibly more glossy and luxuriant in illustration than in life. If Maud has been made to look villainous, then, by contrast, Nash's agreeably open countenance is striking. He is described as softly spoken. He barely raises his voice, his delivery is even and a little weighed down by long suffering. For example:

> In January [Maud] was learning the violin and in order to annoy me at night she would practise. On the night in question I hid the violin and told her to leave and I would give it to her in the morning. She went out and got the axe and proceeded to smash the piano. After this she refused to allow me to come inside the house. She used scissors to keep me out.

It is hard to believe that Maud could have intimidated Nash to this extent. Clearly her counsel thought so too.

'Do you expect this court to believe that a big hefty man like you was knocked about by a little woman?'

'There's no one who can conceive what she's like unless they've seen the woman. She's a maniac.'

Asked what kind of man is the petitioner, Maud replies, 'Most violent.'

'And you have heard it said that you have a violent temper too?'

'Yes, many times,' [wearily].

'And have you?'

'One may be driven to extremes.'

~

One afternoon I left the shoe factory to walk up to Manley Terrace in Newtown, where Maud smashed the piano and chased Nash out to the street with an assortment of knives and scissors. It took about twenty-five minutes. I found the house, evenly covered in frost-white paint. Its front windows gazed darkly back at me. Manley Terrace turns out to be a cul de sac tucked away out of the path of the nor-wester and the colder southerly. The bay windows confront the street flush with domestic pride. The upstairs veranda has been closed off. In Maud's day it must have offered a lofty stage for the lady of the house. Across the road, the brick stables have been renovated into a tasteful townhouse. Around the corner, in Colombo Street, the two-storey houses are from the same Victorian vintage, but a lesser breed. Terrace houses, cheek by jowl, each one with a stoop. At the bottom of the sloping street begin the worker cottages that stretch north and south.

Maud and Harry Nash's house offers grandeur. But its aspect is limited. It wishes to face the street—and no more. There is the feeling of arriving in a bigger world as you turn into Colombo Street, and recoiling from the same as you enter Manley Terrace. The familiar geography of the city lies beyond Colombo, in the direction of the Newtown shops. And northwards, past the hospital, Mt Victoria rises in its hopeless and endless quest to touch the silver underbellies of the planes rising and descending from Wellington airport. In Maud's day Mt Victoria had been scrubbed clear, and the streets sloping up the hill were lined with old wooden houses, some on a lean like a stack of wood waiting to be brought inside out of the weather.

In Manley Terrace I looked for the window Nash dangled

Maud out of. I probably looked like a thief. In a way I was exactly that—I was looking for something to take. I had half a hope that old ghosts would suddenly appear on the doorstep. But the effect of the white paint is clear. The house does not wish to stand apart. It did not want to hang onto the history that had passed through its doors.

~

The police who showed up there regularly never suspected that the cause of the violence and commotion in the Nash household was a child and what she represented. The police never suspect because at such moments Nash is transformed into the respectable businessman. He is the reasonable one, anxious to placate the situation. Once the police depart, the madness resumes.

Very likely Maud is mad, but not without cause. There would be something wrong with her if she were not driven out of her mind by Nash's determination to get rid of her child. By what hideous set of rules must her daughter be evicted as soon as Eric and Ken are born?

But as time goes on, the abuse shows no sign of ending. And I wonder if Maud's resolve weakens. I wonder if her thoughts take her by surprise, thoughts that, at first, smell of betrayal, almost catch in the throat, but also serve the purpose of opening up a possibility. What would happen if she were to do what Nash is bullying her to do? What would that world look like without the presence of the child to provoke him?

Nash is more forthright, more out in the open with his thoughts. If Betty could just disappear the world will be a happier, saner place.

It is the dark side of the imagination taking over. For the moment, Maud's resolve holds.

Nash destroys photographs of Maud's friends and family in England. He forbids her to communicate with them. On one occasion he dresses her down for stopping in a city street to speak with a friend. The arguments continue. The name-calling returns, frequently erupting into violence. At her wits' end, Maud capitulates. It seems that the only way to hold onto her daughter is to reveal the identity of the father.

The moment she names my mother's father, a threshold is crossed. There is a wait to see how the cards have fallen— badly for Maud, as it turns out, because at Nash's insistence she writes O.T. a letter, that is, she takes down what Nash dictates: a demand for money.

~

Maud told the court that Nash made her blackmail O.T. and his family:

> One suggestion was to expose him to the neighbour-hood where he lived, which, incidentally would have meant exposing her [Mrs Evans]. Eventually he came to the conclusion that the best revenge would be to extort money from the man and eventually at his dictation

and under coercion I wrote for £70 to have the child adopted.

The letter Maud wrote to O.T. in August 1917 isn't in the file. So there is no way of knowing how Nash made her frame the request, although Maud did call it 'revengeful blackmail'. O.T. replies immediately, anxious to contain the situation.

> Dear Maude [*sic*]
> I just received your letter today as I have been away, and it knocked the life completely out of me. I am absolutely astonished by the tone in it. Whatever has gone wrong that you are so despondent. You told me you were getting married and your husband was adopting the child so I cannot understand what is the matter. If you write at once you can send it to me direct as I am at home alone. I am quite willing to do whatever I can for both you and the little one. Tell me what is wrong and what you want, and I will do it at once if I possibly can. But do please spare my poor old father and mother if you can. I don't care what I suffer as I know I have sinned, but for God's sake don't do anything desperate. Send at once direct.

Maud replies:

> Dear Mr Evans,
> I can go no longer with Betty living in the same house, so that to get her adopted to someone who would love her and bring her up nicely as well as give her a name is the only way I can get happiness for her…

Nash later writes separately to O.T. enclosing a receipt for the money received. He writes with a pseudonym. He signs his letters H. Manley.

In the summer of 1917 the attacks on Harry Nash—which the court will hear about and the newspapers will leap on with glee—resume.

Nash is cutting the hedge. Maud is watching him from the porch. There is nothing wrong with the hedge, but Nash is cutting it all the same. He is imposing his will on the hedge. As usual he wants the world to conform to his desire, his needs. He does not care about anyone else. He makes the cutting of the hedge appear so reasonable. He would cut off the head of the little girl if he had his way; he would move methodically along the row and cut off her head without a second thought, mindful of process and appearance, mindful of himself and all that he might represent in the eyes of others.

There is something unacceptable about Nash, something so revoltingly present in the man that she cannot abide it any more. It is hard to say whether it is located in any one thing, although his breeches annoy, and the stuffy way he stands in his boots, and his sanctimonious air with the hedge-clippers. She gets up from the porch, almost without a thought other than her revulsion for all that Nash stands for, and it is suddenly necessary to do something to prevent him reaching that place along the hedge where he will harm her daughter with his thoughtless clipping. Something has to be done. And so Maud brings her foot back and kicks Nash in the crotch.

But did the incident actually occur? Nash says that injuries he sustained from Maud's attack put him in bed for a week and that the doctor was called for. The doctor remembers attending Nash, but not at that time, and not for a kick to the crotch, but for a side strain.

If it did happen, then for a split-second Maud must have felt that some justice had been restored. It is hardly a legal argument. It is an emotional one, but this is the nature of her war with Nash.

Maud removes the photographs of Nash's children and his late wife from their frames, presumably to make Nash understand what he is demanding of her, and to provoke him to imagine himself into that space. And to know that if he is abusive to her little girl she will be the same towards his children. And if he dares her into violence, as slight as she is, she won't disappoint.

~

O.T. has sent more money, as per request, but only after a second terse note instructing him how much and what the money is for. Life has become intolerable and Betty cannot continue to live in Nash's household. The money is to pay for Betty to be separated from her mother.

Maud writes, 'Fifty or sixty pounds should do it.' In 1917, fifty or sixty pounds was the average household's rent and food for a year.

O.T.'s money duly arrives—much of it handed to a solicitor who makes the arrangements for my mother to pass out of Maud's world. But in the course of managing the transaction the solicitor dies and, Maud told the court, rather than put herself through the ordeal with a new solicitor, she decided to adopt my mother 'through friends'. She does say 'through' rather than 'to'.

Dr Robertson who treated Maud around this time described her in a note tendered to the court as:

> ...a physical and mental wreck. She was very depressed. She gave the impression of something worrying her mind. She was not a strong woman. There was no evidence of insanity. She was in almost an hysterical condition. I attended her for an acute abscess under the chin, and had to give her a general anaesthetic because of her nervous condition. I considered her condition was due to some mental strain behind it all...I had a conversation with the nurse who merely indicated family trouble.

Another practitioner, Dr Couzens, recalled treating Maud for 'nervous depression'.

~

One of my mother's earliest memories, according to my sister Pat, is driving in Nash's car. It would have been a treat, watching the spray fly off the rocks around the south coast, never guessing that the two people sitting in the front have already plotted another future for her.

The trips in the car turn out to coincide with a brief period when Maud and Nash separate. Maud is six months pregnant with Ken, Nash's second child. But something is afoot. There is a change in Nash. He is accommodating and generous. He pays the rent on a cottage for Maud in Seatoun, a beachside suburb in the city's east and provides her with a weekly income. During this sunny period he builds a house at Rona Bay, across the harbour in Eastbourne. At the weekend he turns up to Seatoun bearing gifts—flowers, chocolates. He has in mind a fresh start, one without Betty. Maud, too, has come round. She has already been through the mill as a fallen woman with an illegitimate child. She is no doubt reluctant to strike out on her own with two—and soon three—small children in tow. And since she is about to sacrifice my mother—and herself—to the greater good, she will stick it out. She will try again.

Several months of grace pass and she moves back in with Harry Nash, this time to the Rona Bay cottage to make a fresh start without the provocative presence of my mother, or the shadow of the child's father that was such a torment to Nash.

Perhaps the damage was already done. In Rona Bay, Maud's grief takes a new turn. She is erratic, irrational. Very likely she is suffering from depression. The old wound festers—there's a return to the tit for tat of the bad old days in Newtown. Possibly it is as straightforward as this: if she cannot be a mother to Betty then she will not be a mother to Nash's children.

She punches Nash's twelve-year-old daughter Marjorie, blackening her eye. The child is forced to move in with friends until boarding school resumes. She throws Nash's son William out of the house into a concrete wall. She smashes another window with a bowl of porridge after an announcement from Nash that he is taking Marjorie away to live elsewhere 'in consequent of her violence'. She throws an iron at Nash who happens to be holding one of the babies; she hurls a music stand at him, she chases him out of the house with a poker, and so on. On the day of the baby's christening she puts a hose down William's back. On Christmas Day she throws a breadboard at Nash and it hits a glass door, smashing it. She then launches at him with a bread knife. The following Easter, on Good Friday 1919 (by which time my mother has been adopted) she attacks William with a lump of wood, driving the boy from the house. She rushes Nash with a carving knife. She chucks pots at him. She beats Marjorie with a copper stick. Marjorie tells of one occasion when Maud entered her room at 2 a.m. and demanded she come out of the house with her. There, after threatening to kill her, Nash, and the babies, Maud broke down and begged Marjorie to get the police. On it goes.

Maud denies most of these charges. Of the attack on the boy she tells the court, 'he just fell over'. And of the broken window—it happened inadvertently while she was 'trying to talk to Nash' and somehow the clothes brush flew into the glass...

And yet, tellingly, in one incident after another—in Manley Terrace and in Rona Bay—when the neighbours intervene it is Maud they take in.

There is also plenty of evidence of violence that for some reason didn't trouble the jury. Dr Couzens tells of finding

> a mark on Maud's forehead, marks of a kick to the left knee, and bruises on her arms, legs and body as though she had been hit and kicked by some person. She told me at the time that her husband had assaulted her and was responsible for her being in that condition.

Testimony from neighbours in Rona Bay recount Maud 'crying and trembling and her blouse torn', and seeing Mr Nash man-handling her and pushing her around.

Nash tries to have Maud committed, but after examining her, a doctor in Rona Bay declares there is nothing wrong with her sanity.

Undeterred, Nash urged a builder to come to the house to look at his wife. Sam Fisher thought she must be sick or had had an accident. He told the court Nash acted like a lunatic, rushing ahead of him and urging him on. After Nash disappeared inside, presumably to haul out the mad woman, Maud appeared at the door holding a carving knife. She said to the builder, 'Look Mr Fisher, this is the one who threatened us with an axe and held it over us since five this morning.' Nash, according to Mr Fisher, did not deny Maud's statement but continued to argue the case of her sanity. 'Look she is a lunatic,' he said. 'She is raving mad.'

> 'I am just as sane as you, Mr Fisher,' replied Maud, 'aren't I?' I said, 'Well, if you are, go and lay down that knife.' She did so immediately. Then Mrs Nash turned to one of the

boys and said, 'He's been thrashing and knocking us about all morning.' The boy said, 'Yes, he has.' Nash made an effort to strike him, but the boy got away from him. Just then Mr Downs jumped the fence and Nash was saying all the time 'how mad she was.' I said, 'Oh, I think it is you who is mad.'

~

What a relief to turn to the farmer's letters, which are civil and generous.

Of course, they are written by a man standing before a window fully aware of the destructive power of the woman outside clutching a stone in her hand. If the letters are civil, they are even more careful not to cause offence. O.T. writes to Nash, aka Mr Manley:

> ...I must apologise to you for addressing your wife by her Christian name, but believe me it was the tone of her letter that made me think she was in dire trouble, and I did not want to shelve the money part, but only wanted to know what really was the matter. I only wish she had explained in her letter and I would have been spared the misfortune of hurting her feelings or yours. I honestly did not want to hurt in any way, and was very thankful to her writing in the way she did. I have worried a lot since I last saw her, but, out of respect for you as her husband and herself, I did not write to her to know if she had got the child adopted. Owing to my father having lost nearly all his money and having given him all spare cash, it is a bit difficult for me

to get all I would like to send at the present moment, but if it will help your wife in a small degree I will send £50 next week and another £50 before the end of the year. I will not forget the child later on and will do something for her when she gets older if it is in my power. I would esteem it a favour if Mrs Nash would reply to this, or just put a few words in to show that you are in harmony in the matter. I still have a great deal of respect for Mrs Nash and will always do my best to help her if she should be at any future time without a breadwinner. Kindly let me know if this arrangement will suit you, and I will forward the money early next week, and the second lot as soon as possible, but not later than the end of the year. In reading Mrs Nash's letter I really thought that she wanted to have the child adopted by strangers and will be thankful if it is the arrangement you are proceeding with. Please let me know what the child's full name will be. I promise that I will not forget to help her if it is in my power in eight or ten years. If you can reply to this so that it will come by Thursday's boat please reply direct to me. In conclud-ing I must thank you both, especially Mrs Nash, for the kindness you have shown me. If there is anything in this letter that causes pain I assure you it is quite unintentional. Yours truly,
Owen T. Evans

PS. Please do not write if you cannot send it by Thursday night's boat.
O.T.E.

In court, it has come down to Maud's word against Harry Nash's. On that score she doesn't stand much of a chance. She is a fallen woman. She reeks of opportunism. She didn't marry Nash because she loved him—a black mark—and sacrificing herself in order to give her daughter a name is not like rescuing a saint from the flames. The word of such a person cannot be held in the same esteem as that of a successful man, generous, perhaps overly generous. It would be hard to believe the jealousy that Maud claims has curdled inside him or her testimony that he is 'a man of very violent temper which he could not control'. It is not easy to believe that he spat in Betty's food and often hit her, or that he threatened to expose the father of the child, or that their frequent changes of address were due to Nash not wanting to remain in neighbourhoods where people knew of his treatment of her.

Ethel Hargrave, who was also paid to look after the children, told the court that 'Mrs Nash was very kind and good to the children. We planned Marjorie's clothes. I never saw her unkind. Marjorie was rather unmanageable and not too truthful.'

Even the assurances of another one-time housekeeper, Mrs Ashworth, apparently lacked sufficient persuasion:

> I had the child, Betty, under my care all the time I was there and no one could have wished for a cleaner child. She gave no trouble. In fact, everyone loved her. She would not go near Nash. I often used to wonder if he had

been cruel to her. She would make friends with everyone but Nash.

The court has a deaf ear by the time Maud is invited to explain herself:

> About two years after marriage Nash was so cruel to the child, and made me so miserable about the matter, and so ill that under the coercion of Nash I wrote a letter to Mr Evans asking for money to have the child adopted…I kept Betty as long as I could but had to have her adopted as there was no hope…About a month after I came back from Seatoun I had taken Betty to friends to adopt her, and I did not want him to know where she was. He returned from Auckland (on business) and instigated Willie to kick me. I sent Marjorie for the constable. Marjorie's statement is not true. He was so violent to me, and Marjorie willingly went, and as usual I was blamed. It was allusions to Betty's father. Nash told people I was mad. Nash hated Betty and me. I have not seen her since the day of her adoption or heard from her adopting parents.

And here is the bit that I wished my mother could have read or heard for herself: 'I only did this as last resort as I loved the child…and wanted to keep it and give it a name and bring it up as one of Nash's family as he had promised before marriage.'

~

Betty nee Seaward turns into Joyce Lillian Fairley. She will live in Island Bay and, later, Petone, where James Fairley had his stationery- and bookshop. Mr Fairley, who my siblings grew up calling Grandad, was, I'm told, a kind and gentle man. The 1918 electoral roll describes him as a 'torpedo man', living at the Shelly Bay naval base with his wife Edith. My sister Pat said he took his own horse off to the Boer War and that on his return he ran a horse-and-cart milk delivery in Island Bay. She remembers his wife, Nana, had an enormous bust, and wore a dress that dropped off the edge of her like a curtain. She liked to play croquet. I imagine they led full lives, but these are the scraps that survive. All I ever knew of Mr Fairley was what was inside that mahogany box containing the past, which my mother had said was difficult to open. I understand he knew nothing of what happened at home when he was at the bookshop, when my mother was tied to a chair and thrashed for her failure to be what the bookseller's wife wanted more than anything, a quick replacement for her own dead children.

In October 1917 the Fairleys lose their daughter, Isabella Margaret, and in April the following year seven-year-old John Fergus 'Jackie'. Later that year, the Fairleys adopt Mum, and name her Joyce Lillian.

She never liked that middle name Lillian. She would smirk whenever asked to supply it on official forms. But Mum embodied the characteristics expected of someone called Joyce. Wore dresses that Joyce would—unflattering dresses—then, after her change of fortune, she dressed more stylishly, and Joyce the bag lady was superseded by Joyce the clothes horse.

—

The house Mum was sent to turns out to be an old rustic timber cottage. Eden Street lies one kilometre up from Island Bay on the edge of Cook Strait. I found the Fairleys' house in a row of wooden houses below the crest of an east-facing hill one December afternoon when fog rolling off the strait had closed the airport and sat in drifts over the hills. A hammer banged away in the unseen distance. The odd car groaned up the steep part of Eden Street from the sea end.

Eight houses along from the Fairleys, the street disappears down a hill. Beyond the nearest neighbour in the other direction the road vanishes. It is an odd piece of landscape, a large sky-basking arena with bits and pieces of hilltop and hillside that sit as if suspended and apart from one another.

When my mother arrived there, Eden Street was the outer boundary of the suburbanisation that had crept up the hill from the Parade. Cattle grazed on the slopes above and on the naked hills across the valley.

I would have liked a tour of the house. I'm not shy about knocking on the door of strangers, so I mounted the steps. But through the front window I saw a woman on her bed reading a book, so I quietly retreated to the road.

The best I could do was to appreciate 88 Eden Street in

relation to everything around it. I noticed those features that might have sprung memories were my mother to have stood where I did—the bullnose veranda on the villa across the road, a number of other rustic cottages of similar vintage, one lovely old place that sat on a knob of hill to the south, a very old and solid cabbage tree that shifted ever so slightly in a steady breeze that poured up the hill where the road dropped from view, and the pitch and roll of a landscape that never really settled into one thing or another.

I followed Eden Street down the steep incline, noting the number of 'No Exit' signs, and very quickly arrived at the Parade on the flat, to a number of two-storey timber shops. Across the Parade I noticed a pedestrian lane running through the back of the houses. The moment I started along it I realised I was following my mother's route to Island Bay School. The lane came out beside a large timber house, possibly a boarding house in Mum's day. On Clyde Street I looked across to the school, where a dad, dressed like an overgrown schoolboy, and his young son raced around the concrete play area on bikes. I crossed the road to read the school's mission statement which was fixed to the fence:

> We are a learning community growing children to be:
> Skilled communicators
> Deep thinkers
> Superb managers of self
> And confident about the future.

The word 'confident' was contained within a star. These are

worthy values. But if I think of them as stars of alignment in my mother's world of 1918 they begin to dim. Her launch pad into the world was altogether different.

~

The bastard is the godfather of the outsider. *Filius nullius*. A Nobody.

A bastard floats free of the normal constraints, but for that freedom a price is exacted—the bastard only ever occupies thresholds. In the Old Testament, the bastard is even more of an outcast: 'He shall not enter the congregation of the Lord, and nor shall his offspring for ten generations.' In the Old Testament the concern is less moral than an anxiety about the weakening of the tribal bond. A bastard in the context of the Old Testament was the offspring of a marriage between an Israelite and non-Israelite.

In *King Lear*, Edmund explains his aloofness from society on the grounds of an 'irregular birth':

> Why bastard? Wherefore base?
> When my dimensions are as well compact,
> My mind as generous, and my shape as true,
> As honest madam's issue? Why brand they us
> With base? With baseness? Bastardy? Base, base?

~

After I read Hawthorne's account of Hester Prynne's shame and the transcript of Maud's divorce in the Supreme Court I felt the world begin to close around me. This is what a greater awareness of the past achieves. It finds a place for everything. Random occurrences—'acts of God'—are exchanged for pattern and inevitability.

Of course the earthquake struck when and where it did, and to the naked eye of course the pattern of bad luck would seem random, unless of course you knew about the old city maps indicating ancient subterranean waterways, and of course I would find myself born into a world of silence because that is precisely what the shamed bestows upon the progeny—a wilful forgetting.

The bastard civilisation rises on its own conceit as 'self-made'. It is as singular as a plant in the desert—luminously present and ducking all questions as to how it came to be there, apparently self-seeding and self-sustaining because there is no other clue to what sprouted it.

~

At 88 Eden Street, the bastard is delivered to a round of new people. There is a new Mum. There is a new Mr Nash. This one is called Mr Fairley. There is a new house, a new bedroom. The windows hold a different aspect.

She is into her fifth year and already there is a growing sense of a life lived and discarded.

The concrete has still to be laid, and when the nor-wester blows, dust rises off the streets. The world is delicate, light. Look how easily it shifts from place to place.

The streets off the Parade are named after rivers—the Derwent, Clyde, Thames, Liffey, Humber. Echoes of faraway places. Echoes of wishfulness.

Memory, in its unbidden way, will bring back the life she knew under Nash's roof—of voices rising up the stairs at Manley Terrace, the sound of someone flung against the wall, Maud's cries and protests. Perhaps a rogue thought—cabbage trees, a craving for something sweet, say ice cream—then the wind in the eaves scurrying the thought, and in the blank space she hears her own name hurled against the ceiling. And she wonders how it is that a name can sound so soiled and beaten about. The guarded inquiries of the neighbours down at the front door. The more forthright voice of the constable. There was that period at Maungahuia in the Wairarapa, where the wind whistled out of sinkholes in the hills and washing flew off the line, and there was the smell of freshly made earth. Perhaps she was just old enough to appreciate that her mother was not of that world.

Of course there are no documents that record the moment of the separation of the mother and her child.

But when the quake struck on 22 February 2011 the city's inhabitants scrutinised themselves, directly, moment by moment. Time was stopped and put up on Facebook and YouTube. The ground shook, and it was recorded by closed circuit cameras, by mobiles switched to camera and whirled about in shaken hands, as well by cooler minds who calmly held up their phones to record the moment of destruction.

There is no footage of the events when my mother's world dramatically changed, or a record of what Maud said to her that last morning. Perhaps it crossed Maud's mind that this was the last time that she and her daughter would wake up under the same roof. This is the last time she will wash her child's face and lace up her boots, or sit her up to the table with a spoon.

I remember taking the dog in its aged, blind state to the vet to be put down. It lay on the vet's table, its tail flat and lifeless, one trusting eye cocked up at me, its muzzle on its paws. And there is another moment too—on the day my mother died. She is sitting in an armchair at home, frail, and every now and then doubling over with stomach pain, but rallying to smile politely up at the woman from the hospice. And just on the edge of my own hearing, so perhaps Mum didn't hear, the woman from the hospice says, 'I think we'll give her another day.' Mum looked interested, as ever wishing to be polite. As it happened she had another 'event' that afternoon. By evening she was hooked up to the morphine drip from which, I discovered, there is no return. Her child-like look of trust haunts me, as does the dog's, and so, now, the terrible feeling of betrayal Maud must have felt as she put out her daughter's breakfast, and later perhaps brushed her hair, and wet a fingertip to remove a crumb from her cheek is easily imagined.

People in Christchurch spoke of the plain everyday

ordinariness that led up to the 22 February earthquake. Then, hours and days and months after the earth shook apart, the mind insisted on going back to when everything held together looking for a sign.

Perhaps a number of little warnings that passed my mother by at the time were later remembered.

Perhaps Maud packed a small suitcase with her things. So it is reasonable for my mother to think she is going somewhere. And then, in small bites, the new circumstances come clear. She is going somewhere. She is going to the Fairleys. And, there they are, standing at the door, smiling down from their adult heights. One tall, the other a pumpkin. The hall is strange too—a different grade of light and air from what she is used to. She follows Maud inside, perhaps to a room where she is invited to play. Time passes. She wonders where everyone is. She returns to the hall. Voices are coming from one of the rooms. She will go there. She pushes on the door, the Fairleys look up, and slowly smile. Her mother has gone.

At the zoo in Newtown she might notice those animals that appear to read our very thoughts and share our instincts. The white feathered cockatoo, for example, with its shifting pink eye. There are other animals that appear homesick or depressed. The baboon reaches up to an overhanging branch and with baffling grace moves off to a remembered corner of the forest. The lions are besieged with homesickness. They are a reminder of everything that is wrongly aligned or out of place.

From the front porch at 88 Eden Street the long view is broken up by stubbly hills and valleys. The fast-moving clouds suggest change afoot, perhaps some rearrangement of the dust at the door where her mother will show up.

She is somebody's daughter. It is hard to say whose. She was Maud's, but now there is another woman who acts like her mother: dresses her, feeds her, but then stares at her as if she ought to be someone else, and is disappointed to discover that she is not that person after all. So she must find a way of living with her failure to be what Mrs Fairley wishes her to be, as well as the failure of what she was in the Nash household.

Did Maud ever visit her daughter? Maud told the court she hadn't set eyes on Betty since handing her on to the Fairleys, four years earlier.

In a letter to O.T. Maud mentions handling the adoption 'through friends'. She doesn't say the friends are adopting my mother. Her vagueness may be deliberate, to prevent Nash discovering Betty's whereabouts. But then why would he care? Wouldn't he be relieved to be rid of the child whom he regarded as a curse on his life, proof of Maud's lying, and of a past of which he was never quite sure?

If the Fairleys were friends, did they cease to be the moment they adopted my mother? If such a friendship survived I imagine Mum would have remembered the bitter-sweet occasions of her mother visiting.

As long as there is memory a life is never fully discarded. It lingers on—a scratch on the ceiling, a corner of the wallpaper pulled away, a whisper, a laugh, a touch, the first lick of something delicious, a ride in a car. And other puzzling moments that make no sense on their own. Mr Nash, who used to cuddle her and at other times call her names, and spit in her food, and shout at her mother, shout at them both as they walked up the street, which made people stop and stare, while others walked on as if they had not heard a thing. And the silences that seem to mean something but she cannot say what it is. The silence building in the car, as they drove at the edge of the strait. Her mother, in the front. Mr Nash looking further up the road. They were on their way to somewhere, but that place has slipped her memory. Why does the mind produce such moments? Where is Mr Nash? Will he find her in his motor car? Perhaps she paints pictures—to reinstate the world she has lost. She puts in a boat, installs her mother as a pilot. The boat is at sea. She paints herself on the beach. Her mother cannot see her, and it seems impossible that the boat will ever turn to the shore where she stands waving. Has her mother lost her? Or is she busy, detained, *preoccupied* with the two boys. These are words she will learn to spell at Island Bay School. She is coming into the complexities of language that will help her establish the arrangement of the world and make sense of it. She is read to. She reads. She wonders where her mother is. What is taking her so long? She learns her mother is in England, which she discovers is on the other side of the world. She picks up a coin. On one side is the King of England. On the other, a tui. She clutches both in the palm of her hand. (As late as 1960, my mother referred to England, where she had never been, as 'home'.)

She may find kinship in the emasculated hills—what once covered them has also gone. The old trees have been replaced. The wind rises to hysteria. People continue to smile. They are encouraged to.

She is awake. Daylight is breaking. It is time to get up, to wash, to eat breakfast, to brush her teeth, to go to school. There are things to attend to, teachers to listen to. Arcane bits of information to store away. Trees weep—a little-known fact. And farmers with an unsentimental eye slit the throats of fly-blown sheep. Beech, she will learn, are happiest in the company of other beech.

~

Solace.

Despondent over the departure of a good friend, Pliny the Younger writes to his correspondent who has offered sympathy, 'Either say something that I have never read of before, or else hold thy peace.'

Cures for melancholia once included conserves of roses, violets, orange pills, condite. 'Odoraments' such as rose-water, balm, vinegar, 'do much to recreate the brains and spirits.'

As an adult Mum swore by her daily tablespoon of cod-liver oil. She also loved to read about other lives, biographies.

Hawthorne introduced the **W** to his name to separate him

from a Puritan forebear, Hathorne, who had been a judge at the Salem witch trials. A slight alteration of name might have succeeded in distancing him, but a writer's works have a way of tracking back to his wellsprings.

Seneca spoke of Simon changing his name to Simonides and setting fire to the house of his birth so nobody should point to it.

In her reading Mum might have found solace in fables. Aesop, for example, telling off the fox and his companions who are complaining for want of tails—'you complain for want of toys, but I am quite blind, be quiet; I say to thee, be thou satisfied.'

And, 'It is recounted of the hares, that, with a general consent they were to drown themselves out of feelings of misery, but when they saw a company of frogs more fearful than they were, they began to take courage and comfort again.'

She loved the sea, found comfort in its moods and inconstancy, in its capacity to reflect and to absorb. As a young woman, she swam between the rafts moored out from Petone Beach. Her swimming course followed the Esplanade and a number of streets running up the valley, named after the ships—*Aurora, Cuba, Tory, Oriental*—that delivered the first white settlers to this same beach. She swam over ghosted moorings. Back and forth, said my father. He maintained she was a good swimmer. Years later, when I was a toddler, she would bring me to this same beach to splash in the shallows, even when the tide was red from the discharge at Ngauranga and the meatworks at the old pā end of the beach. But I never saw her swim.

Krapp's tragedy is that he is stuck with his life. Confined to his tapes, endless replays and outbursts of rage. Maud's strategy was to forget, and to help the process she sought a physical solution. In 1919, some months after she gave up my mother, Maud approached a lawyer to begin separation proceedings. Nash talked her out of it, and persuaded her to spend some time 'with her people' back home.

Maud left in 1920 and returned to England. Two years later she sails back to New Zealand as if arriving for the first time. It is a retracing of an older journey, in the same way as my sister Lorraine would set out from the house after a fit of epilepsy, or, like the basilica on Barbadoes Street, a dismantling followed by a reassembling, so that with the crossing of oceans and the passing of time everything might be stitched back together as good as new. And on her return, Maud will learn to abide within herself.

But not quite yet. There is the tail-end of her marriage to Harry Nash to work through.

They had written to one another over the two years Maud was away. Harry Nash sent a letter off with each boat. Maud's letters arrived regularly. 'Some of Maud's mail was nice enough,' Harry Nash noted, but, 'some of it could be nasty.' In the one letter that survives, Maud calls Nash a liar and accuses him of backtracking on his promise to provide her and the children with a living income while in England. After Nash shows no willingness to pay for her return fare Maud marches off to the New Zealand High Commission in London to demand that the government take an interest in her domestic affairs. More unpleasantly, she threatens to tell Nash's business colleagues in England of his 'appalling treatment' of her.

In England she lives in the house in Taunton where years later I would visit Mavis. Meat and fruit, she complains, are unaffordable, yet she takes herself off to the London theatre and treats herself to extravagant new clothes.

For her passage back to New Zealand she borrows from her brother, Bert. After their departure is delayed a fortnight following a collision in the Channel, Maud and the boys are handsomely compensated with an upgrade to a first-class passage. Six weeks later she passes through the familiar weather-beaten heads of Wellington Harbour.

Things don't get off to the best of starts when Nash is late getting down to the wharf to meet Maud and the two boys off the SS *Paparoa*. Harry's first conciliatory act was to take Maud and the boys to Kirkaldie & Stains department store for morning tea. In Nash's account, within a short time Maud is nagging him.

The next day they make plans to go to the races. They squabble over some slight thing. Within three days of cohabitation Nash has moved out. There has been another incident.

In Maud's absence Nash has employed a housekeeper, a Miss Andrews. I wonder if Maud sniffed the possibility of a dalliance between the housekeeper and Nash. If true, this has a certain poetic justice. If it isn't true then there is no acceptable explanation for what follows.

Mr Nash: 'Mrs Nash and myself had agreed to go to the races with a party. Miss Andrews came down to help and Mrs Nash chased her upstairs, and had Miss Andrews pinned on the bed...'

Miss Andrews: 'Mrs Nash chased me up the stairs and into my bedroom and she tried to throttle me from behind and as I could not free myself I screamed for Mr Nash, and when he freed me I left the house without packing.'

And Nash files for a decree of separation.

~

The judge directs the all-male jury to find one party guilty of cruelty to the other. If it finds both Nash and Maud to be equally guilty of cruelty then he will not grant a decree of separation.

The jury returns in Nash's favour.

Maud appeals on the grounds that the judge unfairly directed the jury, but also to clear her name of all the damaging things Nash said of her in court.

Nash mounts his own lawsuit against one of the Newtown neighbours, Harry Cobb, after he was seen acquainting himself with a number of jurors in a way that Nash felt was prejudicial to his case.

All six Supreme Court judges dismiss Maud's appeal. Judge Stout is especially damning:

Is there evidence in which the jury could reasonably have come to the conclusion that she had been guilty of cruelty to her husband? In my opinion the evidence was ample. I go further and say that if the jury had found her not guilty of cruelty that verdict would have been against the weight of evidence and a perverse verdict.

~

Maud never did come to the front door or appear in the window of her house to wonder about the mysterious car parked along the street.

Maud will never again marry or, as far I know, enter into another relationship. She will raise the two boys on her own. She begins a women's clothing business, which struggles.

Mysteriously, when Mum is around the age of twelve or thirteen, she is plucked from the Fairleys and returned to Maud to live in the building in High Street where, years later, we would buy my school uniforms.

Why? If she knew, Mum never explained. It remains a mystery. Just as puzzling is why the Fairleys would agree.

It's possible that my mother was proving a handful. She told my sisters that after she moved with Maud, Eric and Ken to a house on The Terrace in the city she was forever climbing out of windows at night and getting into trouble. What kind of trouble? It was never spelt out. Mum told her children different things.

From Barbara I learnt that Maud disapproved of Mum's table manners—said she ate 'like an animal'. I wonder if Maud's objection conceals a more painful truth. The little girl she had loved and given away in order to secure her a loving home has turned into someone less loveable than the child she remembered.

In an attempt to escape the past Hester undoes the clasp that fastens the scarlet letter A around her neck and throws it to the ground. The burden of shame and anguish passes out of her. Feeling herself liberated she lets down her hair, her mouth softens, and a radiance returns to her eyes. 'Her sex, her youth, and the whole richness of her beauty came back from what men call the irrevocable past.'

Except, perversely and cruelly, in her newly liberated state she is no longer recognisable to her little girl. She has turned into someone else. For Pearl, the figure of motherly love is burdened and stigmatised, and so, aware of this sad fact, Hester has no choice but to reach down and reattach the scarlet letter.

Perhaps my mother and Maud had moved too far apart, and failed to recognise one another. Their reunion is unpicked and Mum is let go a second time and never again invited back into Maud's life.

Both Maud's sons go off to the Second World War. Ken is a naval officer. Eric returns from the disastrous Crete campaign with memories he will not speak of (and, on the few occasions we met late in his life, whenever I attempted to steer the conversation in that direction he would see it coming and with an evasive smile reach for his glass of gin). He farms land in the rugged central North Island King Country that has been broken in, cleared back to bare lumps of hillside dotted with sheep.

As Maud was a regular visitor, I wonder if the smells of one farm ever brought back memories of Taruna, and of Owen T. Evans, and of the child they had. Did she ever consider these gaps in her life—and reflect on what she had lost? Or had she absorbed the ability to forget?

To look ahead, one must forget. The rules of progress are written into the landscape.

~

In the 1960s, when she was still in her mid-twenties, my sister Pat knocked on Maud's door. At the time Pat worked in the market-research department of the Wills tobacco factory in Petone. She was in charge of a team conducting a door-to-door survey, and when Maud's name came up on the sheet of addresses my sister decided to take that one for herself.

She knocked on the door, and waited. She knocked again. She was about to give up when a woman in her seventies appeared from the side of the house. She had been gardening out the back. Finding the young researcher on her porch, Maud invited her inside. She made my sister a cup of tea and sat her down at the kitchen table.

Pat discovered Maud to be a polite and carefully spoken old English lady. Maud got out her photographs and proudly showed Pat her sons and grandchildren. Then she sat down and put on her glasses and answered the tobacco company's questions without ever knowing that across the table from her sat her granddaughter.

~

The last Maud saw of my mother was when she told her never to show her face again. But Mum remained in Maud's orbit right up to the end.

In 1977, Mum and my sister Barbara followed the cars leaving Maud's funeral service to a house in the beach suburb of Waikanae on the Kapiti Coast. They parked out on the road, and sat there for a while. Mum, as usual, was riddled with self-doubt and old fears. At Barbara's encouragement and insistence, eventually she made herself get out of the car, cross the road, and knock on the door.

Ken Nash recognised her immediately. Fifty years had passed since he had last seen her. He invited her in, but remained formal, distant. Fortunately, Eric was more welcoming. He seemed to know what Mum was after, and to his great credit he willing gave it. He invited her to stay with him and his wife, Barbara, in Warkworth, north of Auckland. After half a lifetime spent apart, sister and brother resumed their relationship. Mum would drive up to Warkworth or else Eric and Barbara would drive down the island to stay with Mum. I remember them sitting on the couch holding hands and, whenever Eric's warm and lovely teetotal wife's back was turned, they would top up each other's gin glass.

Towards the end, when neither one could travel, communication was difficult. Eric suffered from emphysema and could not breathe without the help of an oxygen tank. A series of strokes had cleaned Mum out of language. On one occasion my sister Pat stood in the kitchen passing phone messages back and forth. She had to make most of it up. Eric died a few months after Mum.

~

I looked in the hairdresser's window once and saw her, wide-eyed beneath a dryer, like someone receiving shock treatment. My father used to say I'd send my mother to the loony bin if I carried on the way I did. I can't remember what I did to cause offence. This recollection has no real role to play. But, it continues to exist, like a card fallen out of a pack, representative of other such moments that fail to add up to anything more. In this way a life sheds itself. It leaves skin on furniture, hair on the pillow. A life reduces to a couple of walk-on parts in other people's recollections. And while some faces may fade, others remain stuck forever like an overbearing portrait glowering down from the walls.

The other day I saw a woman in her fifties get up from a cafe table and embrace a younger woman who appeared to be her daughter. Maud never knew her place in Mum's life.

She might have thought to break the ice, perhaps say

something nice. Offered a cup of tea instead of turning the young mother away from the door.

I was thirteen years old when Apollo 8 delivered a wider view of where we lived. How humbling to behold our blueness as never before seen and the extreme vanity of our undertakings and devotions, as well as our fears, of death, and of shame.

SIX

ON THE FIRST real day of summer I flew down to Christchurch, picked up a rental car from the airport and drove into the city. I parked in the shade of the trees above the Avon, then crossed the road to the Bridge of Remembrance and, out of habit, stood where I had in the winter, between the two imperial lions, beneath the inscriptions of old campaigns fought in Messines and Palestine and Mesopotamia.

I barely recognised Cashel Street from the ruins of my last visit. The barriers had been taken down, but I did not shift from the old position. City birds hopped over a vacant site where in June had stood a building I'd seen knocked witless by the swinging arm of a demolition crane. An office desk and chair had raced towards one another in a mad comic embrace before the floor on which both depended crashed to the street in a cloud of dust. The pink insulation of the building flopped out, like the false grin of the dead dog in Stellin Street all those years ago.

I remembered what others had said about the tremendous noise of glass bursting onto the street hours after the earthquake. I thought of the young mothers I'd seen with their prams in a street near Eureka filling water bottles from a huge bladder parked on the side of the road, and of the shiny green human-waste disposal units and portaloos that popped up everywhere, and the new phrases people invented in their darkest moment of need—Stay away from the trees!—as a road rolled up like carpet. 'It's like living with a tyrannical old bitch,' someone said. Did he mean the earthquake or the compassionless landscape? And the tree that stood on the periphery of the devastation, completely unmoved. Likewise the feckless skies. Heartbreak. There is no telling when or where it might strike. When my marriage ended I was amazed to discover, after years of consci-entiously constructing it, just how pot-holed my life suddenly appeared. I thought of the small groups of stunned people I'd seen over that winter gathered at building sites—silence written all over their faces—at a time when there was still talk of rebuilding the city and no one dared say otherwise for fear of being singled out as a shit.

I remember the cries of defiance, and the morale-boosting efforts of self-appointed angels who swept through neighbour-hoods at night painting messages of hope on fences and the sides of buildings. Sentimentality, like weeds, is always first to flourish. But there could be no going back. At the time, my wife urged me not to be rash. Which was tantamount to asking me not to be myself. We were sitting in the car in Jackson Street, Petone. The world moved by in slow motion. People appeared and disappeared and shifted along like fish in an aquarium. We filled the car with our separate silences. One of the ongoing jolts is the daily reminder that what was once always with us is no longer. I spared a thought for the Japanese student buried in foreign rubble. The battery on her cell phone running low while she chose her last words to say to her loved ones in Tokyo. As a child I liked to stick my finger into the gap between my front teeth. The first morning I woke alone in the shoe factory I patted the bed beside me—just to be sure. It was shocking really. A shock—followed by calm afterwards, but only after. The finger probed the toothy gap. I remember I sank back to my side of the bed with a placid moon expression, amazed at the sudden redundancy of the expression 'my side'. Whole buildings—now missing. Imagine it. And for days after, when there was just the echo of myself in the new place, I tiptoed about like a thief.

It was exhilarating to leave the bridge. It was like having freedom of movement back in a leg that has had the plaster removed. A sunny lightness extended all the way up Cashel Street to its colourful shops made out of shipping containers which were huddled around the old city retail establishment of Ballantynes.

Most of us were pretend shoppers, sticking our noses into the showroom, which accounts for me buying a Bavarian sausage in a roll that I didn't really have an appetite for from a woman at a wurst stand.

While she turned the sausage on the grill we talked about the earthquake. She and her husband, a gymnastics coach, were from Hungary. They had arrived just before the September 2010 earthquake. I said something about bad timing, but she was quick to say how much they liked it here. The broken city was now their home, and in spite of everything they had found a way of accommodating the disaster in their lives.

I wandered back to the car, drove past the airport, and carried on north, past the roadside tree stumps brutally cut almost to ground level. Sun-split and weathered, they continued to launch themselves at the sky, held back by roots that carried on in the only way they knew how.

I was on my way to explore the world of O.T., Owen Tibbott Evans.

~

I have a photograph of a wheat field. It could be Russia or the south of England. In fact, the picture was taken by a photographer from the New Zealand Department of Tourism in 1917. Stooks of wheat surround a horse-drawn cart on which sits a man in a hat and a dark suit. Using a zoom I can bring up the white of his collar, but then the face of my mother's father, the North Canterbury farmer, disappears into a haze.

I am his descendant, or more accurately, as I have come to think of it, I am a descendant of a moment of lust and desperate loneliness.

There is no reason to believe that the farmer's other descendants know anything about my mother. Or whether they will welcome the information I bring. They have their own well-tended history to consider, their own family myths to respect. There was that sign I saw in Bexley, one of the areas worst affected by liquefaction—someone had painted on their fence 'We still live here!'

No one likes to think of their life as spectacle.

On the other hand, fault lines do not think. They are indifferent to what has been built on the surface of the earth. Fault lines have their own history to consider. They are not random events, but contain their own inevitability.

It was just a matter of time before I would get in touch with the farmer's family.

Maud may have held the stone but she never cast it, and so O.T.'s family never found out about Betty.

O.T.'s grandson, Wylie Evans, was gobsmacked when he heard about Betty from John Harper, a local historian whom I had taken into my confidence. Harper then got in touch with me to say that the Evans family would like to meet me.

I followed up with an email to Wylie, and one year after the earthquake I found myself retracing Maud's footsteps from the scullery end of the original Evans homestead.

~

This is what happens to a house left on its own to fight the elements. The front roof hangs over the veranda like a bad toupee. Half the veranda has disappeared—into firewood, no doubt. Two huge lateral branches from a bordering macrocarpa lean on the roof with the weight of a drinker's arm.

It is four o'clock at the tail-end of a lacklustre summer, and inside, the house is dark and dank. The tall windows with their old-fashioned pulleys cast just enough light. A torch would be handy because in the hall I have to balance myself on floor joists left exposed by missing floorboards. The floors in the other rooms are intact but covered in sheep shit and dirt. In each bedroom of peeling wallpaper is a fireplace.

Ruins such as this are commonplace on farms where the need to occupy the same site as the original dwelling is not as pressing as it is in the city or on a suburban street where one footprint must be instantly filled by another. So a house is abandoned to the status of an old tree stump or rusting car wreck.

I'm surprised and delighted at how much remains. School exercise books dating back to the 1920s that belonged to Gwendoline, daughter of O.T. and Maggie, lie on the floor. I brush the dirt off a small card from *The Book Society, 13 Grosvenor Place, Hyde Park Corner, London SW1*. There are books by the score, disintegrating in boxes, some scattered over the floors. I pick up *King Solomon's Mines* by H. Rider Haggard. Inside the cover I find it inscribed: 'To Owen Tibbott Evans, Christmas 1896, from Father.' I hold in my hand a book once held by O.T., and his father, and feel an unexpected rush of pleasure.

In a dark cupboard I find three pharmacy bottles dispensed by E.P. Shier, Amberley, in 1923. The bottles have a milky residue, like milk of magnesia, with a labelled instruction to take four times daily. Milk of magnesia is excellent for heartburn, dilutes the fire. I know this from personal experience.

Then I pick up *The Boarding School Girl* and find inside the name of O.T., this six-foot-something, broad-shouldered stockman and stud master.

On a wire spike I find a year's worth of invoices for 1938. I peel off each one, hoping to find something private scribbled in the margins, or a letter that somehow has become muddled up with the bills. But the wire turns up only invoices. Still, something of the man and how he lived is revealed in what he's paid for in the course of the year: bills from Meat and Wool in Marion Street, which is the street abutting Ghuznee with the music store on the corner across the road from the shoe factory, an invoice from the Little Company of Mary Hospital in Bealey Avenue, Christchurch 'for Miss Evans, Rm 23', an invoice from Blackburn Motors in Christchurch, distributors for Buick, for an oil and grease and a pint of shock absorber oil, a receipt for £10 from the New Zealand National Party (to be expected), fees to the Canterbury Park Trotting Club, the Timaru Trotting Club, the Oamaru Trotting Club, invoices for the transport of horses to these meetings (I've since learnt that O.T. won the New Brighton Cup with a horse called Beckleigh). I pull another fistful of invoices off the wire. There's one from Whitcombe & Tombs booksellers, and, devastating for any father to receive, an invoice from Shaw and Sons in Rangiora to cover the funeral expenses for his daughter, Gwendoline, which is unceremoniously followed up with bills from baling and chaff-cutting contractors, hardware merchants, ironmongers, regular invoices from a florist in Christchurch and D.H. Fisher 'Terms Monthly Storekeeper Hawarden', often for the same items: sixteen eggs, cheese, matches, twine.

I wonder which room Maud slept in. Very likely the one nearest the scullery. But perhaps not—I have just learnt about the existence of fourteen-year-old illegitimate May sent 'into service' at Taruna at the same time that Maud lived here. May's bedroom would have been the one nearest the service end of the house, in which case, I decide, Maud must have taken the bedroom directly behind O.T.'s. Great swathes of peeling wallpaper hang down like bats' wings from a pink-flower frieze. Its delicacy has survived the general dereliction of the room.

Hawthorne invoked an onion to describe seduction as a kind of unravelling.

> You may strip off the outer ones without doing much mischief perhaps none at all; but you keep taking one after another, in expectation of coming to the inner nucleus…It proves however, there is no nucleus, that chastity is diffused through a whole series of coats, is lessened with the removal of each, and vanishes with the final one which you supposed would introduce you to the hidden pearl.

Add to that the creaking silence of the house, and a gathering sense that the world has forgotten Maud and O.T. And the casual thought that comes and goes, first as a shameful surprise, and then not at all, but familiar, and then a wish, and then a frustration, and then a need that cannot be suppressed any longer.

Is that what happened? Who would know? Who would possibly know? The trees? The night looking in the windows? The dying embers in grate? The furious stars blinking impotently in the window? The world that might tell is mute. But if we know anything at all about the human condition, then we do know.

My mother was born in December, so she was probably conceived in the early autumnal days of March. The scorching firebrand light dying in the sky. Night air tangy with old fruit lying beneath the trees in the paddock on the south side of the homestead. How strange it was, how extraordinary, to stand in the room where my mother was conceived, and to breathe in the sooted air of this old ruin where the conditions of my childhood—absence, silence, repudiation of the past—were cast.

~

Scratching around in the dark and dirt on the floor of May's room I find novels belonging to her, as well as an exercise book filled with poems by Gwendoline who, I'm told, loved to write and ride horses. Gwendoline died at the age of twenty, officially of leukaemia, but Margaret Evans, Wylie's sister, suspects hydatids was the cause of death. On the floor by a pair of ancient waders I find a volume of *Sacred Songs and Solos* with Gwendoline's name inscribed, and a novel, *Stella's Fortune* by Charles Garvice, enormously popular in its day, with May's name handwritten inside, Mary Olive Kinley.

Apparently May had no other family. Wylie Evans isn't sure where she hailed from—Christchurch, he believes, or possibly Rangiora. All that is reliably known about May is that she was illegitimate. On that fact alone May's persona rests.

In Wylie's recollection, May was always there, working in the background, almost one of the family. After Maggie died, May stayed on, not that there was anywhere else to go. She had grown into Taruna and Taruna into her.

Apparently there was no one else in May's life. She never married. No one came calling, and O.T. always made sure she stayed inside the house whenever a swaggie came in the gate. I'm told he didn't like women to be left alone in the house.

Shearing gangs came and went. The shearing sheds are up the back of the farmhouse. A shearer might have stood in the shade of the shed towelling the sweat off himself and seen May hang out the washing or picking fruit, moving through the shadowed and lit patches beneath the trees surrounding the house. But no one can recall such a scene. Wylie remembers May shouting up the hall for his grandfather to shift his bones before the porridge grew cold.

I wonder about May—the facts of her life recall that basic

need to love and to be loved. She'd been flung out and taken in, like a dog from the SPCA.

May is in Christchurch with Maggie and her new baby Geoffrey, when Maud moves in to Taruna as housekeeper. After Maggie dies, in 1943, May moves into the armchair by the fire and sits into the evening with the farmer. Perhaps O.T. cannot think of May in any other way than as 'service', or even as 'illegitimate', in which case he has saved her. She is forever the fourteen-year-old who arrived out of the blue. I imagine he felt an affection, even a love for this woman who will never leave the property.

On her birthday he will have a present for her. He will rest a hand on her shoulder, plant a chaste kiss on her cheek. It may cross his mind that he has been here before. There was Maud, and he nearly paid dearly for that, worrying himself silly that word would get out.

There was Maud, but where is she now? With Nash? And the little girl, Betty? Whatever happened to her? Is there someone out there who looks a bit like him? Before a blazing fire on a winter's night with May, does his mind wander? The body stirs in the old familiar places. Funny how memory and flesh are so closely linked. He looks across the fireplace to the woman in the armchair. How bright her face looks, almost flushed.

There are sheep to move, to shear, to crutch. There are horses to breed. Race meetings to attend. There are birthdays and wedding anniversaries to celebrate. The birthday of his daughter Gwendoline comes and goes; perhaps it is too unbearable to dwell on. Then, after a period of time, perhaps not. In the weeks and months following his daughter's death, did he find himself wondering about that other girl, Betty?

He remembers his promise to look after her educational needs, and he acts accordingly—paying for his 'sin' as he saw it. Presumably he sent the money to Maud. In which case they must have stayed in touch. Or, more likely, Maud kept that Rangiora post office box address for when the moment came to remind O.T. of his promise.

The post office still has its thickly painted fire-engine-red postal boxes. I stared at P.O. Box 3—that is what it came down to. I stood where he had all those years ago, I imagine in a calmer state than he had. When he died in 1959 I was four years old. I don't imagine he knew anything about me or my siblings. But you never know. I'm inclined to extend to him the privilege of knowing because, half a century later, there I stood, in his old footprints, my eyes set in the same direction as his, occupying a moment that surely he never imagined the future would deliver—an unacknowledged grandson, as I am, aware of his secret.

Maggie passes away three years after Gwendoline—two blows in quick succession. And then the war and its noise, which diminishes personal suffering. The nights continue—no avoiding them. He will sit up with May. May is good company. She knows him and his habits. She knows his breathing when he is asleep. She knows things about him that even he doesn't know. And for those moments that come between them, a silence or a bit of silliness, when they want to fill the room with something other than themselves, parked in the corner is the pedal organ record-player.

O.T. dies, aged eighty. The obituaries mention his success at horse and sheep breeding. Twelve days later, May dies.

In the Horsley Downs Cemetery, a few graves along from O.T. and his son, Geoff, lies May, 'loved friend of the late O.T. Evans and M.A. Evans and family'.

~

I find myself thinking about the cattle that stood against the ridges as they waited for their new home to the west to be cleared by men in hats wading through the smoking Spaniard grass. A century later this is the landscape I drive through, with Harper at the wheel. The road is as straight as a needle, and those foothills which have always stood on the edge of time begin to rear up with surprising haste. Out the side windows is the flat unyielding pasture. It is the same countryside that welcomed Maud all those years ago. I take more care than I usually would to look and note things. The big things—the alps, of course, belittling and at the same time uplifting, the skies forever streaming overhead, and the concentration of self that comes with yawning space.

We slow down for the bridge, clap across its timbers. Below, a river flat is filled with sun hats and colourful beach towels and sparkling water. Children clinging to inflatable tubes float around a bend and out of sight as we come off the bridge onto a bumpy shingle road.

We are travelling through land also abandoned by grand ideas. Harper says there were once plans to build a railway line connecting this valley with the West Coast. The land was surveyed but the railway never eventuated. Old surveyor pegs still crop up in the tussock. As for older footsteps, Maori took this same route through the alps to the west coast. At some point along this dusty road, Harper judges that we have seen enough and turns around. For the second time that day we cross the bridge, this time without looking down, and fly past the gates leading to Taruna. At the church we turn north and carry on a short way to the small country cemetery.

It is quiet, and the late afternoon heat has knocked the stuffing out of the day. The car doors crack as we get out. I can hear the distant noise of a tractor, but nothing else intrudes. Behind us the mountains are still, watchful. We stop by the graves of two teenagers done up like children's playpens. There are toys and flowers, and rocks painted with messages from friends and family. A chair has been placed next to each grave for the visitor to sit and chat with the deceased.

O.T.'s undecorated grey slab, on the other hand, represents another era with its grim austerity. There are no fine words or biblical passages inscribed on it. Information about the deceased is plainly stated. Trotting and shooting are his recreations listed in the *Who's Who* for 1938, as well as a bit of other biographical information. On leaving school O.T. worked at the Central

Dairy Company in Addington, Christchurch, for four years. Then for a number of years he worked at a threshing plant in the Kaiapoi district. In 1902 Messrs Evans & Sons acquired Clifton, a farm of 2500 acres. The picture of the wheatfield taken by the Tourism Department photographer was of Clifton in 1917.

In Hawarden there is an old church with the name Evans scratched into the concrete of its foundations. These days it is a museum. Amid its stifling air and farm implements dating back to the time Maud arrived at O.T.'s farm, Harper dug out a wedding photo.

O.T. looks solid and dependable, but he also looks like any other groom—all personality has been scrubbed from his face for the moment that he and his new wife present themselves on the steps of St Andrew's.

Vainly I search his face for clues to my own, but cannot find a way past the obstructing factors of the smart suit, the carnation, the dutiful, checked smile.

Then Harper showed me a photograph of Richard Evans, O.T.'s father, and I was amazed to find traces of myself—the eyes, the mouth, the thin smile. It was a great surprise, especially recognising those facial features that suggested a kind of muscular pull and take on things. It was as though I had come upon a replica of myself, a bit like Christchurch's old stone edifices built to resemble an older model. I have never felt more unoriginal than at the moment I looked upon Richard Evans.

Harper told me that Richard Evans' father was the sheriff of a village in Monmouthshire, Wales. I wasn't surprised, not the slightest. Some long dormant computation of personality was confirmed. A sheriff? Well, of course it makes sense—and explains those occasions when it befalls me to tell the drunks in the alley beneath the shoe factory to kindly piss off and take their empties with them. I may even get some of that from Dad, who had the same tendencies to present himself as an unlikely figure of authority—coat and scarf and bristling eyes to cover up the fact that he could barely talk—and to rise to his feet in a rugby crowd to remonstrate with a drunk over his use of 'language'. I would crawl deeper inside my collar, in spite of the fact that I was vaguely proud of him getting to his feet to do what others seated around us were too scared to do. But that pride only ever came later, in a quieter reflective moment. At the time I wished he would sit down and shut up. Now, I find myself doing the same—parting a crowd to go to the aid of someone having a seizure. The crowd always responds favourably and I ride in on some assumed authority. The crowd's unquestioned acceptance of my role continues right up until I kneel to ask the prone person if he or she is all right, and then I sense a shift in the air and the unspoken thought that they—well, anyone—could have done that (ask someone if they are all right), and clearly I am not the doctor they took me for, not even a relative, but, it seems, a distant relative of a sheriff in Wales, acting on ghostly initiative.

Richard Evans, Mum's grandfather, experienced respiratory problems in his youth and when a doctor recommended he leave Wales and move to a more agreeable climate, instead of sensibly setting off for Brazil, he travelled to New Zealand, arriving in Lyttelton around the time the swamps identified on the 'black map' of 1854 were drained for the city to extend its boundaries.

He wasted no time in making his way in the world. He established the flour mill at Kaiapoi, a large brick building on the banks of the river, which was partly damaged in the September 2010 earthquake. He took an active role in local politics. He chaired the Waimakariri River Board, and was active in the Methodist Church.

The sheriff's son enjoyed a long and productive life until the fatal day in 1921 he crossed the railway line in Kaiapoi to talk to some men at the timber yard, as he had on other occasions. This time he failed to hear the train's approach and was hit from behind—scooped up by the cattle catcher. His leg was cut off.

O.T.'s brother, Llewellyn, was first on the scene. He told the coroner, 'When I saw him after his accident he said, "This is a bad business, my boy." I asked him how it had happened. The reply, "Well, I really can't say."'

Years earlier, in 1902, Llewellyn went to Wales where he managed a brick-manufacturing plant in Rhyl. He played hockey for Wales, winning a bronze medal at the 1908 Olympics. After his return in 1912 he managed his father's flour mill in Kaiapoi.

But it is his brother O.T. in whom I recognise certain aspects of myself—the way he holds himself is like my own stiff bearing, all the tension rising to the shoulders. Modesty prevents him from showing more than a prim satisfaction. I think that would explain his facial constraint, together with the flattening out of high emotion that comes to those in late middle-age. O.T. has the unfussy grave that he would have wished for.

The sun is low and fierce, and stupidly I've forgotten to bring a hat. I have to hold a notebook up to my eyes to pick out the dark and spare outline of Mt Tekoa. I assumed it is a Maori placename. But Harper corrects me. He says it is from the Book of Amos.

Later that evening I read in the Old Testament about Amos who was among 'the herdsmen of Tekoa…two years before the earthquake…' It turns out to be a depressing sermon on man failing his duties to himself and to God. Amos was a sheep and cattle dealer, a native of Tekoa.

All the way to the alps is sheep farming country, and so perhaps it is not so strange to name a crag after the birthplace of a shepherd from the Old Testament. I wonder if the daily sight of the crag ever set O.T.'s mind wandering. The deeper meaning of Tekoa would not have been lost on him. Just as the Maori meaning of Taruna—'connected'—is not lost on me.

~

It does not feel so long ago that at Wylie Evans' house I sat in O.T.'s rather uncomfortable armchair, the same one he used to occupy by the fireplace in the old farmhouse, and I watched on an early home video a ghost—the father whom my mother never saw and a grandfather I never knew—hover into astonishing proximity.

Suddenly there he is—the shock of white hair, a suit, a dark vest, a white collar, a white handkerchief stuffed into his breast pocket. He wore the same suit day in day out, through summer and winter. 'If it can keep out the cold of winter it can keep out the heat of summer,' he used to say. Wylie passed this on to me. Some words can come from anyone. Other words shuffle out of personality. *If it can keep out the cold of winter it can keep out the heat of summer.* It was like hearing a voice from the grave.

The Buick has been down to Christchurch for a spray paint and O.T. has driven it back to the farm. He pulls over outside the house, the one I had wandered through that afternoon, pacing the rooms, interrogating the walls. There, beyond the rose bed, he parks and gets out. A bit wobbly in the hip. But he is seventy years old. He wears a dark hat. White hair as blunt as a spade hangs out the back. He is in his dark suit and the vest, and there is the white handkerchief. He has no idea that he is being filmed; no cause to suspect it. This is the first time he has been captured on film. His son, Geoff, was among the first in the district to own a movie camera. I wonder what my mother would have made of this moment as the grandchildren—Wylie, Bruce and Margaret—swarm around the car. It is clear that Buick has a status in the family. It is up there with a prize Corriedale. The Corriedale is a curious-looking breed. Its face is narrow, like that of a poodle, bursting out from an enormous shagpile of fleece. Later in the film, O.T.

holds a Corriedale against his legs. I am more interested in the detail of O.T.'s face than the sheep's, but it is hard to make out his face in the shade of his hat and the smoke from his pipe. The sheep gazes up at him and then I see the 'clear face' and 'the straight back' and the 'big bum' that I am told characterises a good Corriedale. This is what it is like to acquire history. You become knowledgeable about things you never expected.

Then I recognise a gesture of my own—a distribution of body weight as O.T. leans against a fence, again, of course, in a dark suit, and hat. And then he appears for the last time, driving a tractor across a paddock. He comes closer and closer into view. One of his grandkids is parked on his lap. He turns his head to look behind at what he has ploughed. And then he is gone.

AFTERWORD

Late one Monday afternoon in March 2013 I returned to the Karori Cemetery with Eleanor Gwendoline Jones's plot number. This time the woman in administration altered her directions— 'turn right at the last street light and look for her in public section 2 next to Hearn and Eliot'. Fallen leaves covered the walking area between the graves and there was a strong smell of eucalypt in the air. I found Eliot, then Hearn, covered in eucalypt leaves. Next door was Eleanor's plot, little more than the collapsed side of a bank. One hundred years after she was interred she at last had a visitor.

ACKNOWLEDGMENTS

Nathaniel Hawthorne's description of the workhouse women on page 195 is from *The English Notebooks of Nathaniel Hawthorne*, Vol II, Riverside Edition, Houghton, Mifflin & Co, Boston, 1883.

The cures for melancholia described on page 236 are from *The Anatomy of Melancholy* by Robert Burton, George Bell & Sons, London.

The land where O.T. Evans once farmed has passed into new hands, and I am very grateful to Jenny and Alex Fergusson for allowing me to poke around in O.T.'s crumbling farmhouse.

I am extremely grateful to the Evans family for their good grace and generosity, and for their hospitality. In a letter circulated to the wider Evans family, Wylie concludes, 'We now all have some relatives of which we weren't previously aware, something I personally think is a bonus.' I concur.

I wish to thank the office of Chris Finlayson, Minister for Culture and Heritage, for putting me in touch with the staff at CERA (Canterbury Earthquake Recovery Authority) who made so many things possible at a difficult time.

Thanks also to Gareth James from Transpacific Waste Management for providing access to the tip operation out at Bottle Lake.

The staff at Archives New Zealand and the Ministry of Social Development showed remarkable patience and I thank both institutions for the documents their searches produced.

To Juliet Nicholas and Ken McAnergney, and Morrin Rout, and Marion Hargreaves, thank you for your hospitality, local knowledge and excellent company in Christchurch. Photographer Anne Noble was a great companion on two trips to the earthquake zone. Christchurch landscape architect Di Lucas generously provided invaluable insight. I am indebted to John Harper who made the initial approach to the Evans family. John guided me around the district and kindly opened the local museum. In 2008, I was fortunate to have Pieter van der Merwe of the National Maritime Museum, Greenwich, guide me through an exhibition of William Hodges' paintings and show me the sketches of the icebergs.

A heartfelt thanks to my first reader and agent, Michael Gifkins, and to my publisher at Text, Michael Heyward, for their tireless efforts on my behalf, and to the wonderful Jane Pearson for her astute and close reading.

Finally, the Russian poet Joseph Brodsky's customary

wisdom, in this instance a line from an essay, kept me on track: 'If art teaches us anything, to the artist in the first place, it is the privateness of the human condition.' From *On Grief and Reason—Essays*, Penguin Modern Classics, 2011, p. 40.